AF266448

UNVEILING THE MYSTERY OF REVELATION

LAGREE CASON

Author's Tranquility Press
ATLANTA, GEORGIA

Copyright © 2024 by Lagree Cason

All rights reserved. No part of this publication may be reproduced, distributed or transmitted in any form or by any means, including photocopying, recording, or other electronic or mechanical methods, without the prior written permission of the publisher, except in the case of brief quotations embodied in critical reviews and certain other noncommercial uses permitted by copyright law. For permission requests, write to the publisher, addressed "Attention: Permissions Coordinator," at the address below.

Lagree Cason/Author's Tranquility Press
3900 N Commerce Dr. Suite 300 #1255
Atlanta, GA 30344, USA
www.authorstranquilitypress.com

Ordering Information:
Quantity sales. Special discounts are available on quantity purchases by corporations, associations, and others. For details, contact the "Special Sales Department" at the address above.

Unveiling the Mystery of Revelation /Lagree Cason
Library of Congress Control Number: 2024914929
Hardback: 978-1-964810-30-0
Paperback: 978-1-964810-31-7
eBook: 978-1-964810-32-4

CONTENTS

Dedication

This book is dedicated to all of my family and friends.

This is the Gospel of Revelation as I believe that it has been revealed to me.

You do not have to believe everything as I believe. I have never walked in your shoes, nor have you walked in mine. God reveals to each of us according to where we are in our walk with him.

You may not consider yourself a learned Bible Scholar, but many of the things that they say and write is only their opinion.

Study the Bible by searching the Scriptures to find the answers that God will reveal to you.

The whole Bible, from Genesis through Revelation is to lead His people to a right relationship with Him, and to accept Jesus Christ as our Lord and Savior.

Author Note: The scriptures quoted in this book are from the New International Version of the Holy Bible.

Credits: The underlined sentences in this book are quotes taken from: **Every Prophecy of the Bible, written by: John F. Walvoord, copyright 1990,1999 by John F. Walvoord, Chariot Victor Publishing.**

Foreword

Problems: Things that human intelligence can eventually work out, such as chess moves, crossword puzzles and worldly things.

Mystery: Something that when the answer is known, human intelligence cannot fully grasp its meaning.

This is why Revelation is considered a mystery. Many cannot or will not believe that Revelation will be fulfilled literally and fulfilled completely as a prophecy. Believe all of the Bible or believe none of it. You do not get to pick and choose. Many people do not read or study Revelation because they do not understand it. They do not understand it because they try to equate "God Power" to man power. Revelation needs to be studied in the exact same context that it is written.

Revelation 1:8 "I am the Alpha and the Omega," says the Lord God, "who is and who was and who is to come, the Almighty."

This one verse should tell us that we should not even think of "God Power" in the same context as man power. There is no way to compare the two.

Genesis 1:1 In the beginning God created the heavens and the earth.

God has no beginning or ending. He is eternal. He took nothing and made the heaven and the earth, along with everything that is in them.

Man, in all of his vast knowledge that God has allowed him to acquire, has never reached out into thin air and grabbed a handful of nothing and made something out of it. Everything that man has made has already had some source that was made by God.

If you want a real comparison of "God Power" versus man power, read the story in **Exodus 13:17 – 14:30**, of God parting the Red Sea and the entire Hebrew nation crossed over on dry land. The Egyptians were the most powerful force in the world at that time. Pharaoh and his army were completely destroyed by God without the loss of one Jew. Man in all of his knowledge even today cannot separate the waters of the Red Sea, let alone do it in one day. **Revelation 1:1 – 3** (1) The Revelation of Jesus Christ, which God gave him to show his servants what must soon take place. He made it known by sending his angel to his servant John, (2) who testifies to everything he saw - that is, the word of God and the testimony of Jesus Christ. (3) Blessed is the one who reads the words of this prophecy, and blessed are those who hear it and take to heart what is written in it, because the time is near.

Revelation 1:19 Write, therefore, what you have seen, what is now and what will take place later.

I do not recall any other prophecy in the Bible in which God commanded his prophet to write down what he saw. All other prophecies were oral in nature, or in a dream or a vision.

I can see God telling John to write down what I am about to show you on my "big screen television". He not only showed John what had happened, what was happening, but what will take place later.

You may say that God did not have a big screen television, but try this: **Revelation 11:1 – 8** God sent two witnesses to witness to the people for 42 months, 1260 days or three and a half years, during the tribulation. After the three and a half years of witnessing, they were killed by the beast that comes up from the Abyss. Their bodies lie in the street of the great city, which is Babylon (which has been rebuilt by the Gentile world rulers).

Revelation 11:9 For three and a half days some from every people, tribe, language and nation will gaze upon their bodies and refuse them burial.

The inhabitants of the earth will gloat over them and will celebrate by sending each other gifts, because these two prophets had tormented those who live on earth. But after the three and a half days, a breath of life from God entered them and they stood on their feet, and terror struck those who saw them. Then they heard a loud voice from heaven saying to them, "Come up here", and they went up to heaven in a cloud while their enemies looked on.

This is a direct revelation of satellite television that has taken man two thousand years to develop. Without some sort of satellite television, it would be impossible for the entire world to view this while it was actually happening. Remember **Genesis 1:1** In the beginning God created the heavens and the earth. There is absolutely no reason to believe that God could not send these pictures across the sky for John to see, if you believe that He made the heaven and the earth in all of its uniqueness and has sustained it forever.

Ever since God made Adam and Eve, man has discovered how to use what God had already made.

If you want another example of "God Power", check out **Revelation 21:1 – 2** (1) Then I saw "a new heaven and a new earth," for the first heaven and the first earth had passed away, and there was no longer any sea. (2) I saw the Holy City, the new Jerusalem, coming down out of heaven from God, prepared as a bride beautifully dressed for her husband.

God did not have anyone to build this city, he commanded it to be and it was. The city was 12,000 stadia in length and it was as wide and as high as it was in length. Twelve thousand stadia is approximately fourteen hundred miles in our measurement. This would cover an area from Tampa, Florida to Boston, Massachusetts, to Minneapolis, Minnesota to San Antonio, Texas and back to Tampa, Florida; pretty impressive city. The streets were paved with gold and it was decorated with every kind of precious stone. **Revelation 21:23** The city does not need the sun or the moon to shine on it, for the glory of God gives it light, and the Lamb is its lamp.

If you believe that God was able to show John the Revelation of all of this, then you have to know that He is in total control of all things.

Revelation 22:18 - 19 (18) I warn anyone who hears the words of the prophecy of this scroll: If anyone adds anything to them, God will add to that person the plagues described in this scroll. (19) And if anyone takes words away from this scroll of prophecy, God will take away from that person, any share in the tree of life, and in the Holy City, which is described in this scroll.

Believe The Book of Revelation as it is written: It is the word of God!!

Chapter 1 – Revelation Chapter 1

Revelation 1:1 – 3 (1) The revelation of Jesus Christ, which God gave him to show his servants what must soon take place. He made it known by sending his angel to his servant John, (2) who testifies to everything he saw- that is, the word of God and the testimony of Jesus Christ. (3) Blessed is the one who reads aloud the words of this prophecy, and blessed are those that hear it and take to heart what is written in it, because the time is near.

The whole Book of Revelation is a message about the sovereignty of God who holds the future of mankind and the world in His hands. Throughout the whole book there is a strong Trinitarian linkage of God the Father, Jesus the Son and the Holy Spirit.

The writings of John are not simply an angel's testimony. It is a direct testimony of Jesus Christ. John wrote as a proclamation of events that was taking place in his present time, and a prediction of God's work in the future. His emphasis was not on secret knowledge and schemes, but on moral living in preparation for the second coming of Jesus.

Revelation 1:4 – 8 Greetings and Doxology. [4]John, To the seven churches in the province of Asia: Grace and peace to you from him who is, who was, and who is to come, and from the seven spirits before his throne, [5]and from Jesus Christ, who is the faithful witness, the firstborn from the dead and the ruler of the kings of the earth. To him who loves us and has freed us from our sins by his blood, [6]and has made us to be a kingdom and priests to serve his God and Father - to him be glory and power forever and ever! Amen. [7]"Look, he is coming with the clouds" and "every eye will see him"; and all the peoples of the earth "will mourn because of him." So shall it be! Amen. [8]"I am the Alpha and the Omega," says the Lord God, "who is, and who was, and who is to come, the Almighty."

God has no beginning and no ending! He has freed us from our sins and has forgiven us so that we can show our love and devotion to Him by praising and serving Him. This is truly how much God loves us.

John 3:16 For God so loved the world, that he gave his one and only Son, that whosoever believes in him shall not perish but have eternal life.

John 14:6 Jesus answered, "I am the way and the truth and the life. No one comes to the Father except through me."

These two verses are the key to understanding the Gospel of Jesus Christ. There is no other way; you must come to God through the redeeming blood of Jesus that was shed on "The Old Rugged Cross", to pay for our sins.

There are five statements in three of the Gospels where Jesus states emphatically that he will return.

Matthew 24:30 Then will appear the sign of the Son of Man in heaven. And then all the peoples of the earth will mourn when they will see the Son of Man coming on the clouds of heaven, with power and great glory.

Matthew 26:63 – 64 [63] The high priest said to Him, "I charge you under oath by the living God: Tell us if you are the Messiah, the Son of God." [(64)] "You have said so," Jesus replied. "But I say to all of you: From now on you will see the Son of Man sitting at the right hand of the Mighty One and coming on the clouds of heaven."

Mark 13:26 – 27 [(26)] "At that time people will see the Son of Man coming in the clouds with great power and glory. [(27])And he will send his angels and gather his elect from the four winds, from the ends of the earth to the ends of the heavens."

Mark 14:61 – 62 [(61)] Again the high priest asked him, "Are you the Christ, the Son of the Blessed One?"

[(62)]"I am," said Jesus. "And you will see the Son of Man sitting at the right hand of the Mighty One and coming on clouds of heaven."

In **Luke** chapter 21, Jesus is telling his disciples what to look for to know the signs the end of time is near.

Luke 21:11 "There will be great earthquakes, famines, and pestilences, in various places and fearful events and great signs from heaven."

Luke 21:9 "When you hear of wars and uprisings, do not be frightened. These things must happen first, but the end will not come right away."

Luke 21:27– 28 (27) "At that time they will see the Son of Man coming in a cloud with power and great glory. (28) When these things begin to take place, stand up and lift up your heads, because your redemption is drawing near."

Luke 21:33 "Heaven and earth will pass away, but my words will never pass away."

This is the only place the word redemption occurs in the Gospels. Our salvation is not yet complete. The complete redemption of God's people will take place at the second coming of Jesus Christ.

Revelation 1:7 declares, "Every eye shall see Him." Many people ask how this is possible. Unlike the rapture, which will take place in the blink of an eye, the second coming of Christ will be a gigantic procession of holy angels and saints from heaven to earth. There is no reason that this cannot take twenty four hours for completion. The earth will make a full revolution in that time frame and every person will witness the second coming of Christ.

Revelation 1:7 ends with "Amen", this means that you can take it to the bank. It will happen! Verse eight; "I am the Alpha and the Omega." These words represent the first and the last letters of the Greek alphabet, meaning that Christ is from the beginning to the end, from eternity past to eternity future.

"The Almighty", is used ten times in the Book of Revelation. When Jesus came the first time He was a baby, born in Bethlehem. When He returns the second time, He will be, "The Almighty", "the King of Kings, and the Lord of Lords." **Revelation 19:16**

Revelation 1:9 – 20 (9) "I, John, your brother and companion in the suffering and kingdom and patient endurance, that are ours in Jesus was on the island of Patmos because of the word of God and the testimony of Jesus. (10) On the Lord's Day, I was in the Spirit, and I heard behind me a loud voice like a trumpet, (11) which said, "Write on a scroll what you see and send it to the seven churches: to Ephesus, Smyrna, Pergamum, Thyatira, Sardis, Philadelphia and Laodicea." (12)I turned around to see the voice that was speaking to me. And when I turned around I saw seven golden lampstands, [13] and among the lampstands was someone like a son of man, dressed in a robe reaching down to his feet and with a golden sash around his chest. [14] The hair on his head was white like wool, as white as snow, and his eyes were like blazing fire. [15] His feet were like bronze glowing in a furnace, and his voice was like the sound of rushing waters. [16] In his right hand he held seven stars, and coming out of his mouth was a sharp, double-edged sword. His face was like the sun shining in all of its brilliance· [17]) When I saw him, I fell at his feet as though dead. Then he placed his right hand on me and said, "Do not be afraid. I am the First and the Last. [18] I am the Living One; I was dead, and now look, I am alive forever and ever! And I hold the keys of death and Hades. [19] "Write, therefore, what you have seen, what is now and what will take place later. [20] The mystery of the seven stars that you saw in my right hand and of the seven golden lampstands is this: The seven stars are the angels of the seven churches, and the seven lampstands are the seven churches."

I do not believe that you will be able to comprehend the magnitude of power and greatness that is revealed in Revelation, unless you can believe that God sent some sort of pictures across the heavens for John to see. I do not believe that God would allow John to continually say that he saw these things that were going to take place in the future, if he did not actually see them.

Verses nine through nineteen is a triumphant appearance of the Risen Lord. As the "Resurrected One", He holds the keys to death and "Hades", the place of the dead.

Jesus Christ is Lord of both life and death. If we trust and follow Him we have no reason to fear death. Death does not hold the last word about human existence. There will be a Judgement Day for all.

Chapter 2 – Revelation Chapters 2 – 3

Revelation 2:1- 7 To the Church in Ephesus. (1) "To the angel of the church in Ephesus, write: These are the words of him who holds the seven stars in his right hand and walks among the seven golden lampstands. (2) I know your deeds, your hard work and your perseverance. I know that you cannot tolerate wicked people, that you have tested those who claim to be apostles but are not, and you have found them to be false. (3) You have persevered and endured hardships for my name and have not grown weary. (4) Yet I hold this against you: You have forsaken your first love. (5) Consider how far you have fallen! Repent and do the things that you did at first. If you do not repent, I will come to you and remove your lampstand from its place. (6) But you have this in your favor: You hate the practices of the Nicolaitans, which I also hate. (7) Whoever has ears, let them hear what the Spirit says to the churches. To the one who is victorious, I will give the right to eat from the tree of life, which is the paradise of God.

Each of these seven churches had an angel, they were viewed as God's messenger to the church.

The church at Ephesus, which was a very prominent city on the western part of the Roman province of Asia, had enjoyed the ministry of Paul for three years.

Acts 20:17 - 19 (17) From Miletus, Paul sent to Ephesus for the elders of the church. (18) When they arrived, he said to them: "You know how I lived the whole time I was with you, from the first day I came into the province of Asia. (19) I served the Lord with great humility and with tears, and in the midst of severe testing by the plots of my Jewish opponents.

Acts 20:21 (21) I have declared to both the Jews and Greeks that they must return to God in repentance and have faith in our Lord Jesus Christ.

Acts 20:28 - 31 (28) Keep watch over yourselves and all the flock of which the Holy Spirit has made you overseers. Be shepherds of the church of God, which he bought with his own blood. (29) I know that after I leave, savage wolves will come in among you and will not spare the flock. (30) Even from your own number men will arise and distort the truth in order to draw away disciples after them. (31) So be on your guard! Remember, that for three years I never stopped warning each of you night and day with tears.

Timothy and John had also served as pastors to the Ephesus church. The church was well established in doctrine and in faith. But, they had lost their zeal for the love of God. They were guilty of a defect of the heart rather than the mind. They knew better, but, they just did not do better. They adopted many of the ways of the world into their life.

Paul urged them to "repent", to change their minds about their relationship to God, and go back to the attitudes which they had characterized previously. The warning to the church was delivered that they would be no longer seen as a lampstand for God, which would give light to other people.

Though God commended them for hating the practices of the Nicolaitans, God still had issues about where they were in their relationship with Him.

It is believed the Nicolaitans were classified as Christians, people who professed faith, but lived licentious lives. I am not sure that I would classify them as Christians. Maybe they were religious, they knew better, but they did not choose to do better.

Revelation 2:8 – 11 To the church in Smyrna. (8) "To the angel of the church in Smyrna write: These are the words of him who is the First and the Last, who died and came to life again. (9) I know your afflictions and your poverty - yet you are rich! I know about the slander of those who say they are Jews and are not, but are a synagogue of Satan. (10) Do not be afraid of what you are about to suffer. I tell you, the devil will put some of you in prison to test you, and you will suffer persecution for ten days. Be faithful even to the point of death, and I will give you life as your victor's crown. (11) Whosoever has ears, let them hear what the Spirit says to the churches. The one who is victorious will not be hurt at all by the second death.

The church at Smyrna was about thirty-five miles north of the church in Ephesus. Ephesus is a deserted city today, but Smyrna is an important port today. It is a bustling city with a population of about 200,000 people. The small church of Christians was opposed and persecuted by the ungodly Gentiles and the Jews. The fact of their suffering then, today and in the future is clearly pointed out in this scripture.

The ten days is probably representative of a short period, but intensive suffering. God was saying to them, "Just hold on for a little while longer and I will rescue you."

Sometimes, suffering is seen as a discipline for things that we have done. Sometimes, it is used as a preventative to keep us from committing sin. Even Christ, though He was sinless, learned obedience from suffering.

Hebrews 5:7 – 9 (7) During the days of Jesus' life on earth, he offered up prayers and petitions with fervent cries and tears to the one who could save Him from death, and he was heard, because of His reverent submission. (8) Son though he was, he learned obedience from what he suffered (9)and, once made perfect, he became the source of eternal salvation for all who obey him.

In the Christian experience, suffering comes before the crown. It is used in scripture as God's recognition of faithful commitment to the Lord.

Revelation 2:12 – 17 To the church in Pergamum. (12) To the angel of the church of Pergamum write: These are the words of him who has the sharp, double-edged sword. (13) I know where you live - where Satan has his throne. Yet you remain true to my name. You did not renounce your faith in me, even in days of Antipas, my faithful witness who, was put to death in your city - where Satan lives. (14) Nevertheless, I have a few things against you: There are some among you who hold to the teaching of Balaam, who taught Balak to entice the Israelites to sin so that they ate food sacrificed to idols and committed sexual immorality. (15) Likewise, you also have those who hold to the teachings of the Nicolaitans. (16) Repent therefore! Otherwise, I will soon come to you and fight against them with the sword of my mouth. (17) Whoever has ears, let them hear what the Spirit says to the churches. To the one who is victorious, I will give some of the hidden manna. I, will also give that person a white stone with a new name written on it, known only to the one who receives it.

The church of Pergamum could be described as a church comprised by the world as many of our churches today. That is, they talked the talk, but they did not walk the walk. They practiced the sins of the world by committing all kinds of sins and living ungodly lives, while pretending to be Christians. The word of the Lord came to the people very clearly to "Repent", which means to turn away from.

The church at Pergamum was established in a city that was mostly pagan and devoted to idol worship. Though the church was in a hostile environment, they were still required by God to bear true witness to Him and they were coming up short. Real evangelism always sparks pressure and problems, but God will always sustain His faithful followers.

In **Numbers 25:1 – 9** A plague struck Israel while they were in Shittim. The plague was blamed on the god of Balaam, who lured Midanite women to entice the Israeli men into eating food that had been sacrificed to idols and committing sexual immorality with them. Christians today can also be enticed to accept local standards of religion that contradicts the gospel. Religion that encourages immorality and lawlessness is Sin.

Revelation 2:16 The words, "the sword of my mouth", represents the Word of God. The Word of God is a double edged sword. It offers the promise of grace and eternal salvation to those who put their trust in Jesus Christ. But, it promises judgement and condemnation to the wicked and the unbeliever.

What was true of the church in Pergamum and their failures and shortcomings, still holds true today. In many churches today, when the world and its value system takes over, it leaves many Christians without much hope.

Spiritual decisions always begin with individuals. The sustaining grace of God is always experienced by those who give their hearts to God. We may be persecuted and ridiculed while here on earth, but we will be rewarded for our commitment and steadfastness to God.

Homosexuality is one of the biggest sins of the world that is running rampant throughout the church today. Some churches are even claiming that it is even sanctioned by God and are allowing their leaders to live in homosexual relationships. Nowhere in the Bible does it say that a man should lie with another man or a woman with another woman.

Genesis 1:27 – 28 [27]) So God created mankind in his own image, in the image of God he created them; male and female he created them. [28]) God blessed them and said to them, "Be fruitful and increase in number; fill the earth and subdue it.

Genesis 2:24 That is why man will leave his father and mother and is united to his wife, and they become one flesh.

All of the court decisions of the world today will not change the validity of God's word. All of these liberal judges and legislators can make any law that they want to, to enhance homosexuality, and all of the smart doctors and scientists of the world will never be able to take male sperm and fertilize another male sperm, of use two women's eggs together to produce a baby.

Homosexuality was one of the main sins that was prevalent in Sodom and Gomorrah. God completely destroyed both cities and there was never a trace found of them again. It is the only sin of these two cities that was actually mentioned by name.

Genesis 19:1 – 29 In verses 1 – 3 two angels arrive in Sodom and are invited by Lot to spend the night with his family.

Genesis 19:4 – 5 (4) Before they had gone to bed, all the men from every part of the city of Sodom - both young and old - surrounded the house. (5) They called to Lot, "Where are the men who came to you tonight? Bring them out so we can have sex with them."

In verses 6 – 9, Lot went outside to try to get them to leave, but they refused. He even offered them two of his daughters who were virgins, but they insisted on having sex with the two angels and kept trying to break the door down to get into the house.

Genesis 19:10 – 11 (10) But the men inside reached out and pulled Lot back inside the house and shut the door. (11) Then they struck the men who were at the door of the house, young and old, with blindness so that they could not find the door.

If God considered homosexuality as a sin in the days of Sodom and Gomorrah, why is it not a sin still today? One of the things that God teaches us when we study His word is; He never changes, He is the same yesterday, today and tomorrow. That is why we can put our trust in Him alone.

In **Genesis 19:12 – 29** The angels tell Lot that he and his family must hurry and leave Sodom because God has sent them to destroy it. God destroyed both cities because of their wickedness, including all of the people who were living in them and all of the vegetation of the land. There has never been any trace of either city found. This was total destruction by God.

Judgement is part of God's history and will be a part of His future plan for the world. God works to eliminate anything that ignores His moral will. Judgement and mercy are both a vital part of God's communication to His people.

God's wrath comes in judgement upon those who do not repent of their sins and turn to Him. How soon that judgement comes and how that wrath is expressed is not for us to decide. Wrath is God's last resort. It is neither right nor loving for God to let sin go unpunished. It is not right because God does not contradict His own basic character by continuing to overlook sin. It is not loving because God will not allow people to have reason to believe that sin is not serious. The fact that God has not dealt with other cities or persons as dramatically as He did with Sodom and Gomorrah does not in any way mean that He will let sin go unpunished.

Revelation 2:18 – 29 To the church in Thyatira. (18) "To the angel of the church of Thyatira write: These are the words of the Son of God, whose eyes are blazing like fire and whose feet are like burnished bronze. (19) I know your deeds, your love and faith, your service and perseverance, and that you are now doing more than you did at first. (20) Nevertheless, I have this against you: You tolerate that woman Jezebel, who calls herself a prophet. By her teaching she misleads my servants into sexual immorality and the food sacrificed to idols. (21) I have given her time to repent of her immorality, but she is unwilling. (22) So I will cast her on a bed of suffering, and I will make those who commit adultery with her to suffer intensely, unless they repent of her ways. (23) I will strike her children dead. Then all of the churches will know that I am he who searches hearts and minds, and I will repay each of you according to your deeds. [24] Now I say to the rest of you in Thyatira, to you who do not hold to her teachings and have not learned Satan's so-called deep secrets. I will not impose any other burdens on you [25] except to hold on to what you have until I come. [26] To the one who is victorious and does my will to the end, I will give authority of the nations – [27] that one will rule them with and iron scepter and dash them to pieces like pottery - just as I have received authority from my Father. [28] I will also give that one the Morning star. [29] Whoever has ears let him hear what the Spirit says to the churches.

Jezebel was one of the most notorious queens in Israel, who led the nation into the immoral practices of Baal worship. The Christians in Thyatira had a similar problem with a woman who was influencing them to commit immoral acts in worshipping idols and immoral sexual activity. Jezebel stands as a powerful reminder of the power of influence of false teachers that are tolerated by the church. Heresy flourishes when sound Christian teaching lags. We today seem to have adopted the policy that if it does not directly involve my family or loved ones it is of no concern of mine.

The New Testament clearly warns people who do not repent of their sins that they will be punished. God the Son is pictured here as the Judge who acts out His perfect wisdom and righteousness.

People who are in positions of power that turn other people away from God's teachings by their deceptive Satanic ways will be dealt with severely by God.

I Kings 21:23 "And also concerning Jezebel the Lord says: Dogs will devour Jezebel by the wall of Jezreel." This was part of what Elijah prophesied to Ahab, the husband of Jezebel concerning the punishment that God was going to bring down on the Israelites for turning to their wicked actions and ways.

Wicked people in the church can appear brilliant by teaching secret knowledge that others have never heard before. When you hear such teachings it must be tested by the scriptures. Too often, these enticing, exciting secrets come from Satan, not God.

The "morning star" is not fully explained but probably refers to a star that appears just before the second coming of Christ, during the darkest days of the second half of the Great Tribulation. It may be a sign to the "ones who overcome" the Satanic ways of the world that help is on the way. Christ will be the one who will return in all of His glory and power at the close of the darkest days of the Great Tribulation.

Revelation 3:1 – 6 To the church in Sardis. [1] "To the angel of the church in Sardis write: These are the words of him who holds the seven spirits of God and the seven stars. I know your deeds; you have a reputation of being alive, but you are dead. [2] Wake up! Strengthen what remains and is about to die, for I have found your deeds unfinished in the sight of my God. [3] Remember, therefore, what you have received and heard; hold it fast and repent. But if you do not wake up, I will come to you like a thief, and you will not know at what time I will come to you. [4] Yet you have a few people in Sardis who have not soiled their clothes. They will walk with me, dressed in white, for they are worthy. [5] The one who is victorious will, like them, be dressed in white. I will never blot out the name of that person from the book of life but will acknowledge that name before my Father and his angels. [6] Whoever has ears, let them hear what the Spirit says to the churches."

Churches as well as individuals can be spiritually dead. Physical life and activity does not necessarily imply that the Holy Spirit is alive and well in a church. Only those that preach the whole gospel can be considered alive. Many churches preach only the goodness of God. They do not preach about the justification of God or of His judgements if you fail to follow Him.

There is a large billboard just north of Alachua, Florida, that is an advertisement for a local church. It says "God is not mad at you, no matter what you do."

Evidently the Old Testament and Revelation must have been left out of their "book of learning". It definitely is not the teaching of the Bible.

God rebukes His people when we stray and calls for us to Repent. Such rebukes are signs of His love. Those who endure the testing and Repent, will receive God's promised rewards in eternity. The reality of the whole world's end and God's judgement calls us to obedience and repentance. In judgement, Jesus will identify His faithful followers before God the Father, and they will be rewarded.

At the time of this letter, Sardis was a prominent city that obtained its wealth from textile and manufacturing, jewelry trade, and the dye industry. Generally speaking, the city was pagan with many individual cults that were very prominent throughout the city.

The church is described as spiritually dead. The message is one of judgement and the warning to Repent. Though the church as a whole was described as spiritually dead, there were a few individuals who were still attempting to serve the Lord. He has promised them and us that He will never blot our names out of the Book of Life.

The Book of Life contains the names of those who are saved through the resurrection of Jesus Christ and He promises to never blot our name out of it. We were bought by His redeeming blood on the cross.

The city of Sardis was located on high ground, surrounded by high cliffs that were very hard to climb. This gave them a sort of feeling that they were invincible, since their enemies could not get to them easily. However, they were invaded two times by armies that did climb the cliffs in the dead of night. God was telling them that He, too, would come upon them in the middle of the night just like the armies did.

We need to very wary of people who say that they have received a new revelation from God. He is the same, yesterday, today, and tomorrow. This is why we can put our faith in Him alone, and not in man. Watch politicians, they tend to tell the people whom they are speaking to at that moment what they think the people want to hear. This is how they get into trouble, by pandering to the people in different sections of the country, by telling them what they think this particular group wants to hear. God tells us what He wants us to hear. The message is the same every day and it never changes. You can depend on God to be true to His word.

Revelation 3:7 – 13 To the church in Philadelphia. (7) "To the angel of the church in Philadelphia write: These are the words of him who is holy and true, who holds the key of David. What he opens no one can shut, and what he shuts, no one can open. (8) I know your deeds. See, I have placed before you an open door that on one shut. I know that you have little strength, yet you have kept my word and have not denied my name. (9) I will make those who are of the synagogue of Satan, who claim to be Jews though they are not, but are liars - I will make them come and fall down at your feet and acknowledge that I have loved you. (10) Since you have kept my command to endure patiently, I will also keep from you the hour of trial that is going to come on the whole world to test the inhabitants of the earth. (11) I am coming soon. Hold onto what you have, so that no one will take your crown. (12) The one who is victorious I will make a pillar in the temple of God. Never again will they leave it. I will write on them the name of my God and the name of the city of my God, the new Jerusalem, which is coming down out of heaven from my God; and I will also write on them my new name. (13) Whoever has ears, let them hear what the Spirit says to the churches."

As the direct descendent of King David, Jesus holds the power to let people into the kingdom of God or He can shut them out.

The name of the city, Philadelphia means, "brotherly love". **Romans 12:10** Be devoted to one another in love. Honor one another above yourselves.

This is kind of like the old saying, "blood is thicker than water". This means that when it comes down to crunch times we will choose our family over our friends and neighbors. The exception here is that the blood is Jesus Christ, and His church is the family. Most of us would choose to die for someone in our family that we truly love. How many of us would choose to die for our neighbor or a beggar on the street. That would be "agape love", the love that Jesus had for us.

I wonder if it is coincidence or an omen from God that in 2007, the city of Philadelphia, Pennsylvania, was named the most dangerous city in the U.S.A. Maybe, it was a message of just how far we have turned from the teachings of the Bible.

In the prophecy to the church of Philadelphia, Christ said, that the people who claim to be believers, but are not, will fall at the feet of the believers and acknowledge I have loved you. The promise is that they will have to admit to their faults in this life or in eternity and recognize the love of God for the church of Philadelphia.

Question: What does a dead atheist and a Christian have in common?

Answer: They both believe in God. When an atheist dies and goes to hell, they find out that there really is such a place and that God sent them there.

The church was also commended for its patience: "I will also keep you from the hour of trial that is going to come upon the whole world, to test those who live on earth." The church of Philadelphia was given the promise that they would not have to endure the terrible judgements of the Great Tribulation that will come upon the world, before Jesus returns to claim His kingdom.

The language is very explicit that they will be kept from the persecution and the great catastrophes that will occur during the Great Tribulation. God promised them that He would protect them and they would not have to suffer during this time. This is the same promise that God made to all Christians through the Apostle Paul.

I Thessalonians 4:13 – 17 (13) Brothers and sisters, we do not want you to be uninformed about those who sleep in death, so that you do not grieve like the rest of mankind, who have no hope. (14) For we believe that Jesus died and rose again, and so we believe that God will bring with Jesus those who have fallen asleep in him. (15) According to the Lord's word, we tell you that we who are still alive, who are left until the coming of the Lord, will certainly not precede those who have fallen asleep. (16) For the Lord himself will come down from heaven, with a loud command, with the voice of the archangel and with the trumpet call of God, and the dead in Christ will rise first. (17) After that, we who are still alive and are left will be caught up together with them in the clouds, to meet the Lord in the air. And so we will be with the Lord forever.

Even though there is some disagreement as to when the "Rapture" will occur, I do not believe that God will put His people through the hell and torment that is promised to take place on earth in Revelation, chapters four through nineteen. I believe that all Christians, God's church will be Raptured before the Great Tribulation. I did not say religious people, I said "Christians." There is "no Christ" in the word religion.

Christianity is God reaching down to earth through His son, Jesus Christ, to save those who believe in Jesus as their Lord and Savior.

Religion is people who are trying to work to be good enough to get to their God. Hindus, Muslims, and Buddhists are mainstay religions of the world. There is no comparison between their religious beliefs and a belief by Christians that Jesus Christ is the Son of God and their Lord and Savior.

In **Revelation 2:12** the reference to the one who overcomes being a pillar in God's temple is the same mode as saying that someone is a pillar of strength in their community. This means that they have garnered respect and trust of the people of the community.

The Holy City, The New Jerusalem, will not be built by man power. It will be commanded by God and come down out of heaven, and each individual will be given a new name that belongs to Jesus Christ.

Revelation 3:14 – 22 To the church in Laodicea. (14) "To the angel of the church in Laodicea write: These are the words of the Amen, the true and faithful witness, the ruler of God's creation. (15) I know your deeds, that you are neither cold nor hot. I wish that you were either one or the other. (16) So because you are lukewarm- neither hot nor cold- I am about to spit you out of my mouth. (17) You say, I am rich; I have acquired wealth and do not need a thing. But you do not realize that you are wretched, pitiful, poor, blind and naked. (18) I counseled you to buy from me gold refined in the fire, so you can become rich; and white clothes to wear, so you can cover your shameful nakedness; and salve to put on your eyes so you can see. (19) Those whom I love I rebuke and discipline. So be earnest and repent. (20) Here I am! I stand at the door and knock. If anyone hears my voice and opens the door, I will come in and eat with that person, and they with me. (21) To the one who is victorious I will give the right to sit with me on the throne, just as I was victorious and sat down with my Father on his throne. (22) Whoever has ears, let them hear what the Spirit says to the churches."

The church in Laodicea could be compared to a business that has gone bankrupt. The outside was beautiful, but inside there was silence. There was no life or work going on there.

Though they did no openly oppose the truth, they did not openly support it either. God kinda equated it to a coffee drinker that poured a hot coffee and forgot about it for a while, then took a sip and found that it was cold. It was the same coffee, but it did not taste the same. The same thing applies to iced tea drinkers who let their tea sit and get warm. It is the same tea, but it does not taste the same. That is the way that the Laodicean church was. They were many of the same people who accomplished great things in the beginning, but now they had no Spirit. They were sort of a meet and eat club, they accomplished very little. Unfortunately, this is true of many of our churches today.

The church was satisfied with being moral, religious, and outwardly they conformed to the description of a Christian life. You could probably equate this to a senior citizen home where there is still life, but it doesn't have much zeal to accomplish things.

There was no indication that they were guilty of gross sins that some of the churches practiced. The problem was that they did not realize that they were spiritually dead. They needed to walk the walk as well as talk the talk.

The word "wretched" was used by Paul to describe himself in **Romans 7:24** What a wretched man I am! Who will rescue me from this body of death?

The word "pitiful" was used by Paul while preaching to the Corinthians on the resurrection of the dead. He preached that if we believe in the resurrection of Christ, we must also believe that we are to be resurrected, because Christ was the first fruit of those who have fallen asleep.

I Corinthians 15:19 If only for this life we have hope in Christ, we are of all people most to be pitied.

Most people in the Old Testament era do not believe in life after death. With the resurrection of Jesus and the preaching of the Gospel, we have a new hope, life after death. Without this hope, life has no meaning.

Our hope in Jesus Christ is for this life and the one that He promises us after this life. In this life we will suffer pain, ridicule and persecution, the same as Christ did, but to a lesser degree. But we know that if we stay faithful that our reward in Heaven will be more than this world can ever offer.

The word "poor" was like being equated to a beggar on the street. They had no spiritual treasures stored up in the "Bank of God".

The word "blind" meant that they were unable to recognize and understand spiritual truth. They were blinded by the ways of the world and could not see the things that God wanted them to do.

They were said to be "naked" because they did not keep their spiritual garments on.

The Laodiceans saw their life the same as the world today sees life, they believed that silver and gold will buy whatever they needed. Christ said that they could buy "refined gold" from Him, which is used in scripture to describe the Glory of God.

The "white raiment" is speaking of righteousness that would cover and protect those that put their trust in Jesus Christ.

The "eye salve" was the preached word of God that would make them see. It would open their eyes to the things that God wanted them to see. In contrast to what the worldly wealth could buy, this was being provided by God and could not be earned or purchased but was supplied by God for those who put their faith in Him.

Many churches today resemble those in Laodicea. They are self-sufficient in the things pertaining to this life, such as fighting hunger, homelessness and other ills of this world. There is no clear exoneration for Repentance that was demanded by God of the Laodicean church. We will be cast out unless we turn to riches that are recognized by God which includes Repentance and service and loyalty to God.

This should be regarded as one of the most powerful verses in the Bible. **Revelation 3:19** Those whom I love, I rebuke and discipline. So be earnest and repent.

The important thing to remember is that His rebuke and discipline stems from His love for His people. If God did not love us so much, He would not care if we were like the rest of the world.

John 3:16 For God so loved the world that he gave his one and only Son, that whoever believes in him shall not perish but have eternal life.

You may love someone enough to die for them, but, could you love someone enough to send your only son to be crucified on a cruel cross? I don't think anyone is capable of this kind of love except God.

If He loves us this much, He has the right to chastise us when we need it. Christ stated the His sole purpose was not to judge, but to bring them to repentance, to turn them away from sin and serve Him.

Paul said in **I Corinthians 11:31 – 32** But if we were more discerning with regard to ourselves, we would not come under such judgement. (32) Nevertheless, when we are judged in this way by the Lord, we are being disciplined so that we will not be finally condemned with the world.

Because "the believers" have established a loving relationship with God, He will not allow us to continue in the sins of the world. Sooner or later in this life or in eternity, we will have to deal with any sin in our life that is unrepented. The great thing about God is once we ask for forgiveness and repent, it is forgiven and forgotten. He is not like us humans who put it in a little safety deposit box to use later to beat someone up with.

Revelation 3:20 "Here I am!! I stand at the door and knock. If anyone hears my voice and opens the door, I will come in and eat with him and he with me."

Christ is saying, "you don't have to look for me, I am right here where I have always been. He is not talking about our salvation here. He is talking about our fellowship with Him, how He will nourish us and how we will grow in the Spirit of God. God does not force Himself on anyone but waits on them to come in faith to receive what He has for us.

Jesus used this same thing in a parable: **Luke 12:35 – 36** "Be dressed, ready for service and keep your lamps burning, like men waiting for their master to return from a wedding banquet, so that when he comes and knocks, they can immediately open the door for him."

This fellowship that God is offering us is more fulfilling and rewarding than any holiday that we can celebrate with our family and friends.

At the end of each of the seven messages, the same invitation was given to those who will listen and receive the love of God.

Revelation 3:21 – 22 "To him who overcomes, I will give the right to sit with me on my throne, just as I overcame and sat with my father on his throne. He who has an ear, let him hear what the Spirit says to the churches."

Christ is saying that His love and fellowship is free to anyone who will hear Him and respond to Him. The great tragedy is that "not many are listening".

The messages to the seven churches represents the major spiritual problems of churches in all ages, even todays churches and tomorrows churches will have these same problems. We humans have short memories and God has to give us a wakeup call now and then. When things are going well in our lives, we have a tendency to get fat and lazy, we forget to give thanks to whom all good things come from.

Let God lead and you follow and you will never need a global positioning system to find the right way.

Chapter 3 – Revelation Chapters 1 and 22

In chapters four through nineteen, John takes us on a journey into what the future of the world will be like just before the second coming of Jesus. I am glad that I am a Christian and that whether I am dead or alive I will be "Raptured" and in heaven with Him when these events take place. "It will be hell on earth."

There are many numbers used in the Book of Revelation. They are 3, 3½, 4, 5, 6, 7, 10, 12, 24, 42, 666, 1000, 1260, 12,000, 144,000, 100,000,000, and 200,000,000. Each of these numbers will be the precise number that God says there are. If He says that there will be seven lamps or seven plaques, this is what there will be. It will not be six or eight, it will be seven. If He says there will be an army of two hundred million, there will not be an army of one hundred million; there will not be an army of one hundred and ninety-nine million. "God can count".

The theme of judgements should convince believers and nonbelievers that a day of judgement is coming. The marvelous pictures of Jesus returning as, "King of Kings and Lord of Lords"; should reinforce our absolute conviction that Jesus is the only way to salvation.

The key to unlocking the mystery of Revelation is found in **Revelation 1:19**. John was instructed: "Write, therefore, what you have seen, what is now, and what will take place later."

There are three distinct time periods that must be separated to gain understanding of what John was seeing.

The "what you have seen" is John having the experience of seeing Jesus in all of His glory while on earth.

The "what is now" is the seven messages that were given to John concerning the seven churches. These messages should be the same messages that our churches today are still preaching and teaching.

The "what will take place later" is the ability of God to let John see what is going to happen in the world in the future.

These events will come to complete fulfillment just as other prophecies in the Bible have already been fulfilled.

There is no literal fulfillment of the prophecies described in chapters four through twenty-two in the history of the world. Therefore, they must be fulfilled at a future time.

One of the important conclusions of this prophecy is that, the "Church of God" composed of all of the "saved", dead and alive will be in Heaven when the events of the "Great Tribulation" and the end of time is taking place. The church in Heaven is in direct contrast to the time of great troubles which will take place on earth prior to the Second Coming of Jesus.

Sixty five times in the Book of Revelation John uses the terms, I saw, I watched, I looked, He showed me, you have seen or you will see. Ten times he goes on to infer that he sees something or that he saw something. Fourteen times John testifies that God or the angel of God spoke directly to him.

This is a total of eighty-nine times that John was in direct contact with God while witnessing the events of the Book of Revelation.

At no time does he say, I had a vision, or I had a dream. You have one of two choices to make. 1, You can believe that God showed these things to John and told him to write them down, or 2, You do not believe that God actually showed these things to John, and you will go to Hell with the rest of the non-believers.

Revelation 22:18 – 20 I warn anyone who hears the words of the prophecy of this Book. If anyone adds anything to then, God will add to him the plagues described in this Book. And if anyone takes words away from this Book of Prophecy, God will take away from him, his share in the tree of life, and in the Holy City, which are described in this Book. He who testifies to these things says, "Yes, I am coming soon."

Chapter 4 – Revelation Chapters 4 – 10

Revelation 4:1 – 11 The Throne in Heaven. After this I looked, and there before me was a door standing open in Heaven. And the voice I had first heard speaking to me like a trumpet, said, "Come up here, and I will show you what must take place after this."

Some people get hung up on whether John went up into Heaven at this time or whether he was on the Isle of Patmos. It does not matter where he was, "the what matters" is the message that God gave him. I, actually like to visualize John sitting on a hilltop on the Isle of Patmos and God scrolling these events on His big screen television, which is the sky. What an awesome display of "God's Power" this would be.

The reference to the voice speaking like a trumpet was to reassure us that God was not speaking a secret message to John. The trumpet was used in the Old Testament to signal the start of many historic battles. God wanted the message to be loud and clear, so everyone could hear and understand.

When we are in tune to God we can have conversations with Him as real as talking to another person. Most of the time it will be God talking and us doing the listening. These times do not happen often, but when you truly need God, He can get very real.

Revelation 4:2 – 11 At once I was in the Spirit, and there before me was a throne in Heaven with someone sitting on it. And the one who sat there had the appearance of jasper and carnelian. A rainbow resembling an emerald encircled the throne. Surrounding the throne was twenty four elders. They were dressed in white and had crowns of gold on their heads. From the throne came flashes of lightening, rumblings, and peals of thunder. Before the throne, seven lamps were blazing. These are the seven Spirits of God. Also, before the throne there was what looked like a sea of glass, clear as crystal. In the center, around the throne, were four living creatures, and they were covered with eyes in front and back. The first living creature was like a lion, the second was like an ox, the third was like a flying eagle. Each of the four creatures had four wings, and was covered with eyes all around, even under his wings. Day and night, they never stopped singing; "Holy, Holy, Holy, is the Lord God Almighty, who was, and is, and is to come!!" Whenever the living creatures give glory, honor and thanks to Him who sits on the throne and who lives forever and ever, the twenty four elders fall down before Him who sits on the throne and worship Him who lives forever and ever. They lay their crowns before the throne, and say, "you are worthy, our Lord and God, to receive glory and honor and power, for you created all things and by your will they were created and have their being."

In heaven all inhabitants testify to God's sovereignty as creator and ruler of the universe. God is the eternal Holy One. God alone has always existed and always will. God alone knows the outcome of history, past, present and future. God rules all things.

What John is seeing is events that will take place on earth and in Heaven after the "Rapture" of all Christians has taken place. The word "church" does not reoccur until **Revelation 22:16**. This signifies that the world will be void of any Christian activities during this time. All individuals, whether Jew or Gentile, are spoken of as individuals who are saved or unsaved.

John's first experience was seeing someone sitting on a throne. The "One" who sat on it had the appearance of jasper and carnelian.

The high priest of Israel represented all twelve tribes of Israel when he performed his priestly functions. On his breastplate, were twelve stones, one representing each of the twelve tribes of Israel. The jasper stone represented the tribe of Rueben, the first born son of Jacob. The carnelian stone represented the tribe of Benjamin, the last born son of Jacob. The mention of these two stones was intended to include all twelve tribes of Israel from the first to the last.

These two names hold a significant meaning. Rueben means "behold the son" and Benjamin means "son of my right hand". Jesus fulfills both of these functions. He is the "Son of God" and He sits on the throne of God with Him on the right side.

The twenty four elders is probably a representative group which represents all of the people. In the Old Testament the priests of Israel were divided into twenty four groups to represent all of the people. The Rapture of the church before the end time events and being judged at the Judgement Seat of Christ is a plausible explanation of those twenty four elders being representative of the church.

Revelation 4:5 "From the throne came flashes of lightening, rumblings and peals of thunder." This scene that John saw was the prelude to the terrible judgements that will be inflicted on the earth before the second coming of Jesus. God used a similar setting to get the Israelites attention when Moses was on Mount Sinai.

Exodus 19:16 On the morning of the third day there was thunder and lightning, with a thick cloud over the mountain and a very loud trumpet blast. Everyone in the camp trembled.

In the Bible, the number seven represents perfection. The seven lamp stands and the seven spirits represent the perfection of Jesus.

Isaiah 11:2 – 5 The spirit of the Lord will rest on him, the spirit of wisdom, and of understanding, the spirit of counsel, and of power, the spirit of knowledge and the fear of the Lord. He will not judge by what He sees with His eyes, or by what he hears with his ears, but with righteousness, He will judge the needy with justice, He will give decisions for the poor of the earth. He will strike the earth with the rod of His mouth, with the breath of His lips, he will slay the wicked. Righteousness will be His belt and faithfulness will be the sash around His waist.

In verse six, the power and clarity of the word of God is represented, "like a sea of glass, clear as crystal."

The sea represents the power whether it is on a calm day when the sea looks like glass or on a stormy day when it can destroy everything in its path. Clear as crystal means that there is no hidden meaning in the word of God, everyone can understand it.

The best relationship to the four animals mentioned in verse seven is to the four Gospels; Matthew represents Christ as the lion or the king. Mark represents Jesus as the Ox, the servant of man. Luke represents Jesus as the man in his human ways. The Gospel of John represents Jesus as the flying eagle. He is above everything, He is able to see and know everything and He is always in control.

The scene described in verse eight through eleven is a look at what Heaven will be like. Everyone will be singing and praising the Almighty God. This will be in direct contrast to the hellacious events that are taking place on earth during the Great Tribulation at this time.

Revelation 5:1 – 4 The scroll of the Lamb. "Then I saw in the right hand of Him who sat on the throne, a scroll with writings on both sides and sealed with seven seals." This scroll was a parchment rolled up on a roller with writings on both sides, a sealed with seven seals in such a way that as the scroll was unrolled, each seal had to be broken successively. "And I saw a mighty angel proclaiming in a loud voice, "who is worthy to break the seals and open the scroll?" But no one in Heaven or on earth could open the scroll or even look inside it. I wept and wept because no one was found worthy to open the scroll or even look inside it. Then one of the elders said to me, "Do not weep. See the lion of the tribe of Judah, the Root of David has triumphed. He is able to open the scroll and its seven seals."

The loud voice indicates that what the angel was saying was very important and that everyone should pay attention and hear what is about to happen.

John wept because he did not think that anyone was worthy to open the seals or look inside. Then one of the elders said to him, "Do not weep! We have someone who is worthy to open the scroll and break the seals. He is the lion of the tribe of Judah and the Root of David."

The reference to Christ as the lion is found in **Genesis 49:9 – 10** (9) "You are a lion's cub, O Judah; you return from the prey my son. Like a lion he crouches and lies down, like a lioness, who dares to rouse him? (10) The scepter will not part from Judah, nor the rulers staff from between his feet, until he comes to whom it belongs, and obedience of the nations is his.

The tribe of Judah was known as the tribe of the lion and was the one from which Jesus would come.

Jesus was prophesied by Isaiah as being a descendant of King David. **Isaiah 11:10** "In that day, the Root of Jesse, will stand as a banner for the peoples, the nations will rally to him, and his place of rest will be glorious." Jesse was the father of King David.

This is the only time that the Book of Revelation refers to Christ as a lion. This is in direct contrast to the many times that he is referenced as, "The Lamb". Jesus is both a lamb and a lion. The identity of Jesus as the Lamb comes from Him being sacrificed on the cross for our sins. He paid it all.

As a lion is referred to as the king of beasts because of its mighty power and the ability to kill or destroy all other animals, Revelation tells us unequivocally that Jesus will return as "King of Kings and Lord of Lords". No one will be more powerful or stop Him from imposing His will on the world. What a glorious day of rejoicing this will be.

Revelation 5:6 – 10 (6) Then I saw a lamb, looking as if it had been
slain, standing in the center of the throne, encircled by the four
living creatures, and the elders. He had seven horns and seven
eyes, which are the seven Spirits of God, sent out into all the earth.
(7) He came and took the scroll from the right hand of him who sat
on the throne. (8) And when he had taken it, the four living creatures
and the twenty-four elders fell down before the lamb. (9) Each one
had a harp and they were holding golden bowls, full of incense,
which are the prayers of the Saints. And they sang a new song:
"You are worthy, to take the scroll and to open its seals, because
you were slain, and with your blood, you purchased men for God,
from every tribe and language and people and nation. (10) "You have
made them to be a kingdom and priests, to serve our God and they
will reign on earth."

The reference to the horns in verse six seems to indicate the authority that a powerful ram would have within a herd of sheep. Sheep are known as docile animals, but I have seen rams fight and they pack enormous power.

The elders are the same twenty-four who fell down before the one on the throne and now they fall down and worship the lamb, which shows His deity and His Lordship.

The King James Version of verses nine and ten may give a better understanding of these two verses.

Revelation 5:9 – 10 (9) "For thou wast slain, and has redeemed us
to God by Thy blood, out of every kindred and tongue, and people
and nation. (10) And hast made us, unto our God, kings and priests
and we shall reign on earth."

This gives a more positive indication that these were real people and not angels, and that they were bought by the "Blood of the Lamb", when He was sacrificed on the cross.

Revelation 5:11 – 12 (11) Then I looked and heard the voice of many angels, numbering thousands upon thousands and then thousand times ten thousand. They encircled the throne, and the living creatures and the elders. (12) In a loud voice they sang, "Worthy is the Lamb, who was slain to receive power, and wealth, and wisdom, and strength, and glory and honor and praise.

This is a pretty impressive number in this choir. Just the numbers ten thousand times ten thousand equals one hundred million, plus the thousands times thousands gives you more than another million. Remember this is "God Power", not human power that John is describing in the future of this world.

Revelation 5:13 Then I heard every creature in Heaven and on earth and under the earth, and in the sea, and all that is in them singing, "To Him who sits on the throne, and to the Lamb, be praise and honor, and glory and power forever and ever." The four living creatures said, "Amen" and the elders fell down and worshiped.

These scenes of worship in Heaven will be in sharp contrast to those taking place on earth during the Great Tribulation. The fact is, that in Heaven there is victory, glory and majesty, and that in God's time, His authority will be expressed on earth. This will happen when Jesus comes a second time to set up His millennial kingdom. He will rule the world for one thousand years.

Daniel had many of these same scenes in his dream in Daniel chapter seven. God is the Ancient of Days and the One who sits on the throne. He has always existed and always will. God's Saints (all Christians). His people will inherit His kingdom and possess it for eternity. Earthly kings have power only temporarily. **Daniel 7:26 – 28** is a prelude to what will take place on earth that John saw in Revelation and wrote about.

Daniel 7:26 – 28 (26) But the court will sit, and his power will be taken away and completely destroyed forever. (27)Then the sovereignty, power, and greatness of the kingdoms under the whole heaven will be handed over to the Saints, the people of the most high. His kingdom will be everlasting, and all rulers will worship and obey Him. (28) This is the end of the matter.

This will happen when Jesus comes the second time. You can put this in the bank. Just as sure as the sun rises in the east every day, the world will see Jesus coming down from Heaven to take control.

Revelation 6:1 – 8 The Seals. (1) I watched as the Lamb opened the first of the seven seals. Then I heard one of the four living creatures say in a loud voice like thunder, "Come". (2) I looked and there before me was a white horse. Its rider was given a bow, and he was given a crown, and he rode out as a conqueror bent on conquest. (3) When the Lamb opened the second seal, I heard the second living creature say, "Come". (4) Then another horse came out, a fiery red one. Its rider was given power to take peace from the earth and to make men slay each other. To him was given a large sword. (5) When the Lamb opened the third seal, I heard the third living creature say, "Come". I looked and there before me was a black horse. Its rider was holding a pair of scales in his hand. (6) Then I heard what sounded like a voice among the four living creatures saying, "A quart of wheat for a day's wages, and three quarts of barley for a day's wages, and do not damage the oil and the wine. (7) When the Lamb opened the fourth seal, I heard the voice of the fourth living creature say, "Come". (8) I looked and there before me was a pale horse. Its rider was named Death and Hades (Hell) was following close behind him. They were given over a fourth of the earth to kill by sword, famine, and plague, and by the wild beasts of the earth.

This period will begin after the "Rapture" and when the world is void of all Christian activity. A ten nation group will emerge out of the Middle East, which will be similar to the United Nations or the European Union, only they will have more power. A leader will emerge who will gain control of three of these nations to be more powerful than the remaining seven nations. In a short period of time he will gain control of the other seven nations and will be recognized as a world leader. Then he will enter into a covenant with Israel bringing peace for the first three and on half years of the Tribulation.

At the midpoint of this seven year period he will proclaim that he is the ruler over the entire world. This will be the beginning of the final three and one half years of the Great Tribulation, when God will pour out His judgements on the world.

The scroll with the Seven Seals now becomes the key to understanding the events which were prophesied for this time. Out of the seventh trumpet will come a series of seven bowls of wrath. These are the judgements God will send on the world preceding the Second Coming of Christ. Each one will increase in severity and be more harsh and punishing than the previous one.

The symbolism of a white horse is a picture of power. Though Christ is pictured as riding a white horse into the world from Heaven, in **Revelation 19:11 – 21**, this is not Jesus. This is the antichrist showing off his power. This is probably the same person that is called the "beast" in **Revelation 13:4**. The question is asked, "Who is like this beast? Who can make war against him? He will be so powerful that no one will dare to challenge him."

The opening of the second seal reveals a red horse which is symbolic of war. There will be a series of wars during the last three and one half years of the Great Tribulation. These series of wars will all end in the Battle of Armageddon when Christ will defeat all the armies of the world.

When the third seal is opened the rider on the black horse is holding a pair of scales to weigh out a person's wages for a day's wages. One of the great perils of war is the destruction of crops and infrastructures which will bring on famine and great hardships.

The fourth seal reveals a pale horse and its rider is named "Death". The first thing that happens when a person dies is they usually turn pale or lose some of their color. The term "you look like walking death" will be very appropriate at this time. War causes hunger, which causes sickness, diseases and plagues. The sword represents death by instruments of war.

Hades is the place that those who are not saved go when they die to await their judgement day.

The world's population is approximately six billion. This means that 1.5 billion people will die at this time. This is more people than in North America, Central America, and South America combined.

Jeremiah 30:7 "How awful that day will be! None will be like it! It will be a time of trouble for Jacob (Israel) but, he will be saved out of it."

Jesus described the Great Tribulation with these words. **Matthew 24:21 – 22** (21) "For there will be great distress, unequaled from the beginning of the world until now, and never to be equaled again. (22) If those days had not been cut short, no one would survive, but for the sake of the elect, those days will be shortened."

These passages of scripture make clear understanding that the world is headed for unprecedented trouble. With all the weapons of war that the world possesses, along with the supernatural "Power of God", those days will be like none the world has ever seen.

Revelation 6:9 – 11 The fifth seal martyrs. (9) When he opened the fifth seal, I saw under the Alter the souls of those who had been slain, because of the Word of God and the testimony they had maintained. (10) They called out in a loud voice, "How long, sovereign Lord, holy and true, until you judge the inhabitants of the earth and avenge our blood?" (11) Then each of them was given a white robe, and they were told to wait a little longer, until the number of their fellow servants and brothers who were to be killed as they had been was completed.

One of the most asked questions about salvation and the resurrection of Christians is, "What is the status of a saved person between the time when he dies an earthly death and the time when he is resurrected?" Scriptures are clear that his soul will go to Heaven immediately, but what will be the status of his body?

This passage, along with **Luke 16:22 – 24** and **Revelation 7:9** states that believers will have some kind of body.

Luke 16:22 – 24 The beggar and the rich man. (22) The time came when the beggar died and the angels carried him away to Abraham's side. The rich man also died and was buried. (23) In Hell, where he was in torment he looked up and saw Abraham far away with Lazarus by his side. (24) So he call to him, "Father Abraham, have pity on me, send Lazarus to dip the tip of his finger in water and cool my tongue, because I am in agony in this fire.

Revelation 7:9 The Great Multitude. After this I looked and there before me was a great multitude that no one could count, from every nation, tribe, people and language, standing before the throne, and in front of the Lamb. They were wearing white robes and were holding palm branches in their hands.

How could the rich man who died and went to Hell recognize Father Abraham and Lazarus from far away if they did not have some kind of body similar to their earthly body when they went up to Heaven? How could the great multitude standing before the throne and praising God and the Lamb, be wearing white robes if they did not have some kind of body to hang them on? The passage clearly states that they were holding palm branches in their hands. Are not hands a part of the human body?

God can probably put a robe on a spirit and have them carry palm branches, but why should He, when He can give Christians new bodies that will last forever?

The sovereign and Holy God will exercise His authority to judge. The picture of God throughout Revelation is that He has the supreme authority and power to hold all people accountable to Him. He will avenge the martyred dead in His judgements, because He is true, just and faithful.

Revelation 6:12 – 17 The sixth seal: Catastrophe Judgements. (12) I watched as he opened the sixth seal. There was a great earthquake. The sun turned black like sackcloth made of goat hair. The whole moon turned blood red (13) and the stars in the sky fell to earth, as late figs drop from a fig tree when shaken by a strong wind. (14) The sky receded like a scroll rolling up and every mountain and island was moved from its place. (15) Then the kings of the earth, the princes, the generals, the rich, the mighty and every slave and every free man hid in caves among the rocks of the mountains. (16) They called to the mountains and the rocks fall on us and hide us from the face of Him who sits on the throne, and from the wrath of the Lamb. (17) For the great day of their wrath has come and who can stand?

God's Judgement or His Grace; Which do you prefer? These things that John is seeing have never occurred as far as the history of the world reveals. These cosmic happenings are associated with God's direct intervention in wrath and judgement on an evil world. God's word contains a powerful warning about the severity of His wrath against wickedness.

It would be very difficult to paint a picture more dramatic or more awful than this one. During this great earthquake, buildings will fall, bridges will collapse, holes in the earth will open up and whole buildings will disappear. The sun will turn black and there will be no source of heat. The moon will turn as red as blood. The stars will fall from Heaven. The heavenly bodies will be shifting around. Every mountain and island will be moving. This will be more of a power display than when He opened up the Red Sea for the Israelites to walk through on dry land. This will be real "God Power". It will happen!!

Jesus, Himself, said that these things will take place. **Matthew 24:9** "Immediately after the distress of these days, the sun will darken, and the moon will not give its light, the stars will fall from the sky and the heavenly bodies will be shaken."

Joel 2:30 – 31 (30) I will show wonders in the heavens, and on the earth, blood and fire, and billows of smoke. (31) The sun will be turned to darkness, and the moon to blood, before the coming of the great and dreadful day of the Lord.

The phrase "the great day" is not a twenty four hour time period as we know a day, but is a period of time over which these events will occur. It could be longer or shorter, only God will know when to end it. "Who can stand" makes clear that only those who respond to the grace of God will have a victorious everlasting life with God. Whether this is fulfilled by the "Rapture", when all Christians will be called up to Heaven, or the ones saved by God after the Rapture does not matter. All who come to God will be saved.

Revelation 7:1 – 8 The martyred Dead in Heaven. The 144,000 of Israel. (1) After this I saw four angels standing at the four corners of the earth, holding back the four winds of the earth to prevent any wind from blowing on the land or the sea, or any tree. (2) Then I saw another angel coming up from the east, having the living seal of God. He called out in a loud voice to the four angels who had been given power to harm the land and the sea. (3) Do not harm the land or the sea or the trees, until we put a seal on the foreheads of the servants of our God. (4) Then I heard the number of those who were sealed; 144,000 from all the tribes of Israel. (5) From the tribe of Judah, 12,000 were sealed, from the tribe of Reuben, 12,000 , from the tribe of Gad, 12,000,(6) from the tribe of Asher, 12,000, from the tribe of Naphtali,

12,000, from the tribe of Manasseh, 12,000, (7) from the tribe of Simeon, 12,000, from the tribe of Levi, 12,000, from the tribe of Issachar, 12,000,(8) from the tribe of Zebulun, 12,000, from the tribe of Joseph, 12,000, from the tribe of Benjamin, 12,000.

Two of the most asked questions about Revelation are: 1, Will anyone be saved during the time of the Great Tribulation? 2, If so, how can they be saved a part from the Holy Spirit, which will be absent at this time?

2 Thessalonians 2:7 For the secret power of lawlessness is already at work; but the one who holds it back will continue to do so until he is taken out of the way. This passage refers to the Holy Spirit being removed from the world at the time of the Rapture. This will allow the wickedness of the world to permeate and flourish without interference from the Holy Spirit. Wickedness and world power will have free reign over the entire world. But, people will be saved! They will be saved by the same methods that God used before the Day of Pentecost, when He sent the Holy Spirit to dwell in the hearts of His people.

This 144,000 that will be saved will all be Jews, 12,000 from each of the twelve tribes of Israel. Throughout the Old and New Testament, one of the tribes was left out because the descendants of Joseph grew so large that it became two tribes. Usually, it is the tribe of Levi that is omitted. This time it is the tribe of Dan, one of the smaller tribes.

Not all Israelites will be saved during the Great Tribulation, only those who come to accept Jesus as the Son of God.

Zechariah 13:8 "In the whole land," declares the Lord, "two thirds will be struck down and perish, yet one third will be left in it."

This 144,000 is seen again in Revelation chapter fourteen where they are seen as the redeemed, pure and blameless, purchased by God. This passage makes it clear that some Jews will be saved when they die during the Great Tribulation and that some will be preserved through to the end of time when Jesus returns to set up His kingdom on earth.

Revelation 7:9 – 17 The great multitude in white robes. (9) After this I looked and there before me was a great multitude that no one could count, from every nation, tribe, people and language, standing before the throne and in front of the Lamb. They were wearing white robes and were holding palm branches in their hands. (10) And they cried out in a loud voice: "Salvation belongs to our God, who sits on the throne, and to the Lamb." (11) All the angels were standing around the throne, and around the elders, and the four living creatures. They fell down on their faces before the throne and worshiped God, (12) saying, "Amen! Praise (1) and glory (2) and wisdom (3) and thanks (4) and honor (5) and power (6) and strength (7) be to our God forever and ever. Amen!!" (The number seven again, perfection) (13) Then one of the elders asked me, "These in white robes, who are they and where did they come from?" (14) I answered, "Sir, you know." And he said, "These are they who have come out of the Great Tribulation; they have washed their robes and made them white in the Blood of the Lamb." (15) "Therefore, they are before the throne of God and serve Him day and night in His temple, and He who sits on the throne will spread His tent over them. (16) Never again will they hunger, never again will they thirst. The sun will not beat upon them nor any scorching heat. (17) For the Lamb at the center of the throne will be their shepherd; He will lead them to springs of living water. And God will wipe every tear from their eyes."

The Gospel is for all people! Everyone can receive salvation through Jesus Christ. All they have to do is accept Him as their Lord and Savior. He died to pay for their sins and He rose again. Salvation is the point of focus for God the Father, and the Lamb, Jesus the Son. Salvation comes only from the throne of God!

John 5:24 – 27 (24) "I tell you the truth, whoever hears my word, and believes in Him who sent me has eternal life; and will not be condemned, he has crossed over from death to life. (25) I tell you the truth, a time is coming and has now come when the dead will hear the voice of the Son of God, and those who hear will live. (26) For as the Father has life in Himself, so He granted the Son to have life in Himself. (27) And, He has given him the authority to judge, because He is the Son of Man."

This was Jesus teaching the multitudes at the Pool of Bethesada. Jesus was saying that you don't have to buy it, or work for it, it is free, it is my gift to you. All you have to do, is believe in me!

There are many interpretations of this chapter who confuse it by making a non-literal happening. If you truly believe in the power of God and all of the things that he has done, there is no reason to believe that this will not happen, just as John wrote about.

The severity of the Great Tribulation and the number of martyrs here indicate that most of those who come to Christ in the end time will be faced with a choice, and a large number of them will be executed for not worshiping the world leader. This passage reassures us of how in Heaven, all of the earth's sorrows will be erased and all of the saved will be the object of God's grace.

The most powerful example of conversion in the Bible is found in
Acts 9:1 – 19 (1) Meanwhile, Saul was still breathing out murderous
threats against the Lord's disciples. He went to the high priest, (2)
and asked him for letters to the synagogues in Damascus, so that if
he found any there that belonged to the Way, whether men or
women, that he might take them as prisoners to Jerusalem. (3) As
he neared Damascus on his journey, suddenly a light from Heaven
flashed around him. (4) He fell to the ground and heard a voice say
to him, "Saul, Saul, why do you persecute me?" (5) "Who are you,
Lord?" Saul asked. "I am Jesus, whom you are persecuting," He
replied. (6) "Now get up and go into the city and you will be told
what you must do." (7) The men who were traveling with Saul stood
there speechless; they heard the sound but did not see anyone. (8)
Saul got up from the ground, but when he opened his eyes, he could
see nothing. So they led him by the hand into Damascus. (9) For
three days he was blind and did not eat or drink anything. (10) In
Damascus, there was a disciple named Ananias. The Lord called to
him in a vision, "Ananias." "Yes, Lord," he answered. (11) The Lord
told him, "Go to the house of Judas on Straight Street and ask for
a man from Tarsus named Saul, for he is praying. (12) In a vision he
has seen a man named Ananias come and place his hands on him
to restore his sight." (13) "Lord," Ananias answered, "I have heard
many reports about this man and all the harm he has done to your
Saints in Jerusalem. (14) And he has come here with authority from
the chief priests to arrest all who call on your name." (15) But the
Lord said to Ananias, "Go! This man is my chosen instrument, to
carry my name before the Gentiles and their kings, and before the
people of Israel. (16) I will show him how much he must suffer for

my name." [17] Then Ananias went to the house and entered it. Placing his hands on Saul, he said, "Brother Saul, the Lord Jesus, who appeared to you on the road as you were coming here, has sent me so that you may see again and be filled with the Holy Spirit." [18] Immediately, something like scales fell from Saul's eyes, and he could see again. He got up and was baptized, [19] and after taking some food, he regained his strength.

To get the full picture of this passage, you need to understand who Saul was. He was not someone riding on a donkey leading a band of no bodies. He was a high ranking officer in the army, probably riding a big black stallion that would have shown power and authority. There is probably a good chance that he even witnessed Jesus being persecuted and hung on the cross.

What do you think was going on in his mind when all of a sudden he was lying on the ground and heard this voice speaking to him, but could not see who was speaking? How do you think he felt as he was being led into Damascus by the men he was supposed to be leading?

Be sure that you understand that the scripture says here, that Ananias and Saul both had visions of what God wanted to show them. This is quite different to John continually saying in Revelation that he saw these things that God was showing him. At no time does he say, "I had a vision."

Why did God say to Ananias, "This man is my chosen instrument."? He wanted to show the people that if he could change Saul from being a persecutor of the Gospel (which means good news) to being a proclaimer of the Gospel, that He could change anyone's life who would let Him come into their heart.

There will be 144,000 Jews that will have a similar experience during the Great Tribulation and they will become witnesses for Jesus. They will be protected by the hand of God with a seal on their foreheads. They will cover all the earth bearing witness to their fellow Jews that they have had a super natural visit from God and now they recognize Christ as the Messiah.

Revelation 8:1 – 5 The seventh seal and the Golden Censer. [1] When he opened the seventh seal, there was silence in Heaven for about a half an hour. [2] And I saw the seven angels who stand before

God, and to them were given seven trumpets. (3) And another angel, who had a golden censer, came and stood at the alter. He was given much incense to offer with the prayers of all the Saints, on the golden alter before the throne. (4) The smoke of the incense, together with the prayers of the Saints, went up before God from the angel's hands. (5) Then the angel took the censer, filled it with fire from the alter, and hurled it upon the earth; and there came peals of thunder, rumblings, flashes of lightening and an earthquake.

This half hour of silence will be like waiting for a jury foreman to read the verdict of a high profile trial, or waiting for the final decision in a highly competitive contest of some kind. Everyone will be paying full attention.

Make sure that you understand that this fire came from the Throne of god. It will be part of His judgement on an evil world.

A local church billboard reads, "God is not mad at you, no matter what you do."

God may not be mad, but He is a just God and He is going to be handing down some harsh punishment on an evil world. If He is not angry at this time I want to be in Heaven when He does get mad and begins to mete out His judgements.

Romans 1:18 – 32 God's wrath against mankind. (18) The wrath of God is being revealed from Heaven against all the godlessness and wickedness of men who suppress the truth by their wickedness, (19) since what may be known about God is plain to them, because God has made it plain to them. (20) For since the creation of the world, God's invisible qualities, His eternal power and divine nature, have been clearly seen, being understood from what has been made, so that men are without excuse. (21) For although they knew God, they neither glorified Him as God, nor gave thanks to Him, but their thinking became futile and their foolish hearts were darkened. (22) Although they claimed to be wise, they became fools. (23) Therefore God gave them over in the sinful desires of their hearts to sexual impurity for the degrading of their bodies with one another. (24) They exchanged the truth of God for a lie, and worshiped and served created things, rather than the creator, who is forever praised. Amen!! (25) Because of this, God gave them over to shameful lusts. Even their women exchanged natural relations for unnatural ones. (26) In the same way men also abandoned natural relations with women and were inflamed with lust for one another. (27) Men committed indecent acts with other men, and received in themselves the penalty for their perversion. (28) Furthermore, since they do not think of it worthwhile to retain the knowledge of God, He gave them over to a depraved mind, to do what ought not to be done. (29) They have become filled with every kind of wickedness, evil, greed and depravity. They are full of envy, murder, strife, deceit, and malice. They are gossips, slanderers, God haters, insolent, arrogant and boastful; they invent ways of doing evil; they disobey their parents; (30) they are senseless, faithless, heartless, and ruthless. (31) Although they know God's righteous decree that those who do such things deserve death, they not only do these very things, they also approve of those who practice them.

It is almost mystifying how some preachers, pastors, teachers, can stand before their congregation and preach and teach that homosexual acts are an acceptable and approved way of life by God. Since the Bible is and unchanging guide for us to live by, it seems that if it was a sin when the Bible was written, it is a sin now.

2 Peter 2:1 – 3, 12, 17, 20 - 22 False teachers and their destruction. (1) But there were also false prophets among the people, just as there will be false teachers among you. They will secretly introduce destructive heresies, even denying the sovereign Lord who bought them, bringing swift destruction on themselves. (2) Many will follow their shameful ways, and will bring the way of truth into disrepute. (3) In their greed, these teachers will exploit you with stories they had made up. Their condemnation has long been hanging over them, and their destruction has not been sleeping. (12) But these men blaspheme in matters they do not understand. They are like brute beasts, creatures of instinct, born only to be caught and destroyed, and like beasts, they too will perish. (17) These men are springs without water, and mists driven by a storm. Blackest darkness is reserved for them. (20) If they have escaped the corruption of the world by knowing our Lord and Savior, Jesus Christ, and are entangled in it and overcome, they are worse off at the end than they were at the beginning. (21) It would have been better for them not to have ever known the way of righteousness, than to have known it and then turn their backs on the sacred command that was passed on to them. (22) Of them, the proverbs are true; a dog returns to its vomit; and a sow that is washed goes back to her wallowing in the mud.

It is quite understandable that the fires of Hell will burn a little hotter when these people reach their final destination.

Revelation 8:6 – 13 The Trumpets. (6)Then the seven angels who had the seven trumpets prepared to sound them. (7) The first angel sounded his trumpet and there came fire and hail, mixed with blood and it was hurled down upon the earth. A third of the world was burned up, a third of the trees were burned up and all of the green grass was burned up. (8) The second angel sounded his trumpet, and something like a huge mountain, all ablaze was thrown into the sea. A third of the sea turned into blood, (9) a third of the living creatures in the sea died and a third of the ships were destroyed. (10) The third angel sounded his trumpet, and a great star, blazing like a torch, fell from the sky on a third of the rivers and the springs of water. (11) The name of the star is wormwood. A third of the waters turned bitter and many people died from the waters that became bitter. (12) The fourth angel sounded his trumpet, and a third of the sun was struck, a third of the moon, and a third of the stars, so that a third of them turned dark. A third of the day was without light and also a third of the night. (13) As I watched, I heard an eagle that was flying in midair call out in a loud voice: Woe! Woe! Woe to the inhabitants of the earth, because of the trumpet blasts about to be sounded by the other angels.

Remember in the Bible the number seven represents perfection or completeness. These trumpets will be heard all over the world and they are sounded to gain everyone's attention that something dynamic is about to happen. These trumpets describe the chronological sequence of the various judgements that are about to be poured out on the world.

The seventh seal in verse one includes all of the seven trumpets, just as the seventh trumpet includes all seven of the bowls of wrath. The effect is that each judgement will come with increased severity and more rapidly in time before the second coming of Christ.

Many people say that it is impossible for hail and fire to be mixed with blood. But, when you consider how much power God can pack in a single bolt of lightning, this can and will happen. Verse seven says that one third of the earth will be burned up. Will this be the same as Sodom and Gomorrah, when God rained burning sulfur on them? God so destroyed these two cities that He did not leave any ashes to be found later.

Remember, in **Revelation 1:10**, God commanded John, "Write down what you see." This is a direct revelation of God, it is not someone's prediction. God's camera can take pictures of the future.

This huge mountain like object that falls from Heaven, into the sea, will be some kind of meteor or maybe even a star like the ones that fell from Heaven when the sixth seal was opened. It will cause huge tidal waves and more destruction than the Tsunami that struck in December of 2005.

Many people say that it is impossible to turn one third of the sea into blood. This is the same kind of thinking that Pharaoh had in **Exodus 7:14 – 21** The Plague of Blood. (14) Then the Lord said to Moses, "Pharaoh's heart is unyielding; he refuses to let the people go. (15) Go to Pharaoh in the morning as he goes out to the water. Wait on the bank of the Nile to meet him and take into your hand the staff that was changed into a snake. (16) Then say to him, the Lord, the God of the Hebrews has sent me to say to you: Let my people go, so that they may worship me in the desert. But until now you have not listened. (17) This is what the Lord says: "By this you will know that I am the Lord! With the staff that is in my hand, I will strike the water of the Nile and it will be changed into blood. (18) The fish in the Nile will die and the river will stink; the Egyptians will not be able to drink its water." (19) The Lord said to Moses, "Tell Aaron, take your staff and stretch out your hand over the waters of Egypt. Over the streams and canals, over the ponds and all the reservoirs, and they will turn to blood. Blood will be everywhere in Egypt, even in the wooden buckets and stone jars." (20) Moses and Aaron did just as the Lord had commanded. He raised his staff in the presence of Pharaoh and his officials and struck the water of the Nile, and all the water was changed into blood. (21) The fish in the Nile died, and the river smelled so bad that the Egyptians could not drink its water. Blood was everywhere in Egypt.

If you believe that God turned the water into blood in the days of Moses, surely you must believe that He can and will do it again. He even turned all of the water that was in buckets and stone jars into blood. This is "God Power"; not man power.

The one third of the ships that are destroyed will be destroyed by the huge tidal wave caused by the huge mountain like object falling into the sea.

When the third trumpet sounded a huge star named wormwood, fell from the sky and turned one third of the rivers and streams bitter and many people died from the bitter water. This is the opposite end of the spectrum from when the Israelites were wandering around in the desert and they found water but it was bitter and they could not drink it.

Exodus 15:22 – 27 The waters of Marah and Elim. (22) Then Moses led the Israelites from the Red Sea and they went into the desert. For three days they traveled without finding water. (23) When they came to Marah, they could not drink its water because it was bitter. (That is why the place is called, Marah) (24) So the people grumbled against Moses, saying, "What are we supposed to drink?" (25) Then Moses cried out to the Lord, and the Lord showed him a piece of wood. He threw it into the water and the water became sweet. There the Lord made a decree and a law for them, and He tested them there. (26) He said, "If you listen carefully to the voice of the Lord, your God, and do what is right in His eyes, if you pay attention to His commands and keep all His decrees, I will not bring on you any of the diseases that I brought on the Egyptians, for I am the Lord who heals you." (27) Then they came to Elim, where there were twelve springs and seventy palm trees, and they camped there near the water.

This is another instance in which you need to know and understand the history lessons of the Old Testament. One of the great lessons of history is, if you do not know the history of something, you cannot prepare for the future. If God turned bitter water into sweet, drinkable water, He can surely turn good drinkable water into bitter poison water. Don't say people won't drink it if it tastes bad, because when your tongue starts to swell inside your mouth from thirst, you will drink anything available.

In this passage God wanted the Israelites to remember the power and mighty force that He used to free them from slavery in Egypt. But, He is also a powerful and just God, when we do not receive

His tender love and amazing grace, this time it will be to punish an evil world.

The fourth trumpet relates to Heaven in contrast to the first three, which were judgements on the earth. The effect that this will have is that the earth will become colder and darker without light from the sun, moon, and stars. This will affect the growing of plants for food for every living creature on earth. These judgements coincide with what Christ predicted in **Matthew 24:21 – 22** (21) "For then, there will be great distress, unequaled from the beginning of the world until now, and never to be equaled again. (22) If those days had not been cut short, no one would survive, but for the sake of the elect, those days will be shortened."

The events of the Great Tribulation will exceed any judgements of the past, or the future. They are catastrophic judgements and we should not try to explain them away. God is the all-powerful God and we should not try to put limits on whatever He decides to do. God is purging the world of evil in preparation for the millennial kingdom of Jesus Christ.

The eagle represents the "Deity of God", no bird flies higher than the eagle and no one is higher than God. An eagle soars effortlessly high above the earth and can see a small mouse running on the ground and swoop down to catch it. God is the same way, He is high above us and sees our every move. "Woe! Woe! Woe!" all Hell is about to break loose. The next three trumpets signal judgements that are worse than the first four.

Revelation 9:1 – 12 The fifth trumpet and first woe. (1) The fifth angel sounded his trumpet, and I saw a star that had fallen from the sky to the earth. The star was given the key to the shaft of the Abyss. (2) When he opened the Abyss, smoke rose from it like smoke from a gigantic furnace. The sun and the sky were darkened by the smoke form the Abyss. (3)And out of the smoke locust came down upon the earth and were given power like that of the scorpions of the earth. (4) They were told not to harm the grass of the earth or any plant or tree, but only those people who did not have the seal of God on their foreheads. (5) They were not given power to kill them, but only to torture them for five months. And the agony they suffered was like that of the sting of a scorpion when it strikes a man. (6) During those days, men will seek death, but they will not find it; they will long to die, but death will elude them. (7) The locusts looked like horses prepared for battle. On their heads they wore something like crowns of gold and their faces resembled human faces. (8) Their hair was like women's hair and their teeth were like lions teeth. (9) They had breast plates like breast plates of iron, and the sound of their wings was like the thundering of many horses and chariots racing into battle. (10) They had tails and stings like scorpions, and in their tails they had the power to torment people for five months. (11) They had as king over them the angel of the Abyss, whose name in Hebrew is "Abaddon" and in Greek "Apollyon". (12) The first "woe" is past, the other two "woes" are yet to come.

The star is apparently an angel who will have the power to open the shaft of the Abyss to let loose the terrible judgement represented by the fifth trumpet.

As John watched the smoke pouring out of the Abyss, he saw locusts coming out of the smoke that looked like scorpions. Though they looked like locust and had the powerful sting of a scorpion, they were neither. They were actually fallen angels of the demon world. They were instructed not to harm anything but the people who did not have the seal of God on their foreheads. If you do not believe in demons, search the New Testament scriptures to see how many times Jesus mentions demons and how many times He cast them out of people.

Some question whether or not people who were saved but did not have the seal of God on their foreheads were tortured. Verse four states that they were given the power to torture those who did not have the seal of God on their foreheads. It seems contrary to God's purpose the He would torture anyone who had accepted Him as their God and their Lord. Therefore, if you do not have the seal of God on your forehead, you are not a child of God. Since this judgement came from God, He would not torture His people.

The first four trumpet judgements took place in a short period of time. This judgement of torture lasted for five months. In tropical climates, where they have large scorpions, they have the power to kill small children and they inflict terrible pain when they sting anyone. Because of this terrible pain, John stated that men will seek death, but they will be kept from it.

The sting of these scorpions will be much more severe than the sting of an ordinary scorpion in our world. Demons and angels can take on appearances other than human and the description of these locusts does not resemble any category of man or beast. This will be a “super natural judgement” manifested by the “Power of God”.

Abaddon in Hebrew and Apollyon in Greek, both mean “destroyer”.

The time period of this torturous judgement will be five months, because that is what John was told.

God’s judgement on the world will be so severe that people will desire death over life. Death is not the worst experience humans face, at times pain and sickness can be worse than death.

Revelation 9:13 – 21 The sixth trumpet and second woe. (13) The sixth angel sounded his trumpet, and I heard a voice coming from the horns of the golden alter that is before God. (14) It said to the sixth angel who had the trumpet, “Release the four angels who are bound at the great river Euphrates.” (15) And the four angels who had been kept ready for this very hour and day and month and year, were released to kill a third of mankind. (16) The number of mounted troops was two hundred million. I heard their number! (17) The horses and riders I saw in my vision looked like this: Their breastplates were fiery red, dark blue and yellow as sulfur. The heads of the horses resembled the heads of lions and out of their mouth came fire, smoke and sulfur. (18) A third of mankind was killed by the three plagues of fire, smoke and sulfur that came out of their mouths. (19) The power of the horses was in their mouths, and in their tails; for their tails were like snakes, having heads with which they inflicted injury. (20) The rest of mankind that were not killed by the plagues, still did not repent of the work of their hands, they did not stop worshiping demons and idols of gold, silver, bronze, stone and wood, idols that cannot see or hear or walk. (21) Nor did they repent of their murders, their magic arts, their sexual immorality, or their thefts.

This golden alter was the same alter that John saw in **Revelation 8:3 – 4** when the smoke of incense together with the prayers of the Saints went up before God. The golden alter was used for burning incense and worshipping God within the temple or tabernacle. The brass alter was used for burning bloody sacrifices outside of the temple or tabernacle.

The voice coming from the horns on the alter was probably the voice of an angel. The four angels who were released refers to fallen angels or demons. Holy angels are never bound, they are free to worship God all of the time. These four angels had been kept bound for this very instant in time when they would be released to kill one third of the remaining population of the world.

If the world population is approximately six billion at the time of the Great Tribulation, which is what it is today, this is what the numbers will look like. The fourth seal in **Revelation 6:8** will kill one fourth of the population. This will be approximately 1,500,000,000 people. Of the remaining 4,500,000,000 people left, the sixth seal will kill one third or 1,500,000,000. These numbers will be in addition to the number of people who die from the other judgements that God sends on this evil world. This will leave less than half of the total population alive after this sixth seal.

The army of 200 million will probably come from China. It is believed that they have more than this number in their military today. It is the only country with enough population and financial resources to support a military of this size. This number was given to John because he could not see and count an army of this size.

The Euphrates River is the eastern boundary of the Holy Land. The coming of this army from the east, where China is located is confirmed by: **Revelation 16:12** The sixth angel poured out his bowl on the great river Euphrates and its waters were dried up to prepare the way for the kings from the East.

When Russia controlled what is now Israel, they built a series of dams along the Euphrates River which makes drying up the river possible.

God may even use His super natural powers as He did when He parted the Red Sea and the Israelites walked through on dry ground. He also stopped the Jordan from flowing when it was at flood stage and the Israelites walked across it to the Promised Land.

However God decides to do it, the army from the East will be able to cross with its war machines into Israel. The Euphrates River has steep banks on both sides, but with the river dried up it will be easy to cross.

Some believe that these horses represent modern warfare such as tanks and armored vehicles. This would be the source of firepower, smoke and sulfur. Sulfur has been used in making gunpowder which gives the smoke a sulfuric smell.

Throughout the Bible, God has used evil empires to chastise or bring judgements on people to have them come to Him to be rescued.

Though the remaining people on earth witnessed the horrors of God's judgements, they still do not change their ways, or repent of their evil deeds. Throughout the Book of Revelation we see the mighty judgements of God unleashed on an evil world. But, we also see the utter contempt and depravity of the human heart when it is untouched by the grace of God. They continue to worship their idols and live in sin.

Revelation 10:1 – 11 The angel and the little scroll. (1) Then I saw another angel coming down from Heaven. He was robed in a cloud, with a rainbow above his head, his face was like the sun, and his legs were like fiery pillars. (2) He was holding a little scroll which lay open in his hand. He planted his right foot on the sea and his left foot on the land, (3) and he gave a loud shout like the roar of a lion. When he shouted, the voices of the seven thunders spoke. (4) And when the seven thunders spoke, I was about to write; but I heard a voice from Heaven say, "Seal up what the seven thunders have said and do not write it down." (5) Then the angel I had seen standing on the sea and on the land raised his right hand to Heaven. (6) And he swore by him who lives forever and ever, who created the Heavens and all that is in them, the earth and all that is in it and said, "There will be no more delay." (7) But in the days when the seventh angel is about to sound his trumpet, the mystery of God will be accomplished, just as he announced to his servants the prophets. (8) Then the voice that I had heard from the Heaven spoke to me once more; "Go take the scroll that lies open in the hand of the angel who is standing on the sea and the land." (9) So I went to the angel and asked him to give me the little scroll. He said to me, "Take it and eat it. It will turn your stomach sour, but in your mouth it will be as sweet as honey." (10) I took the little scroll from the angel's hand and ate it. It tasted as sweet as honey in my mouth, but when I had eaten it, my stomach turned sour. (11) Then, I was told, you must prophesy again about many peoples, nations, languages and kings.

God is the eternal creator who brought everything into existence. God controls the destiny of the universe. He alone decides when the day of judgement will be. God does not forget His promises. He is faithful to the end. What He first spoke through His prophets in the Old Testament will come to pass. God's people can depend on Him. Delay does not mean forgotten.

The description of the angel is very graphic. He is robed in a cloud with a rainbow above his head, and his face is compared to the brilliance of the sum. His legs are like fiery pillars. His right foot is on the sea and his left foot is on the land, which requires supernatural power to stand with one foot on the sea and one foot on the land.

When the angel spoke, he gave a loud shout like the roar of a lion. When this happened the seven thunders spoke up and John was about to write down what they said, but he was told not to write this down.

This mighty angel makes the important announcement that there will be no more delay. The time for choosing God is now while you still have the choice to make.

John was informed by the angel that when the seventh angel is about to sound his trumpet, "the mystery of God will be accomplished." We are not capable of understanding all of the things that God does. Nor, does God expect us to understand all that He does.

The King James Bible translates this verse this way: **Revelation 12:7** But in the days of the voice of the seventh angel, when he shall begin to sound, the mystery of God should be finished, as he hath declared to His servants, the prophets.

If God did not tell His prophets "how" He was going to accomplish all the things that He said He would do, why should we get hung up now on how He accomplished these things or how He will accomplish all of these future events.

The theme of Jonah being swallowed by a fish should not be about "how" big the fish was, but about "why" the fish swallowed Jonah.

Personal Miracle: I was sitting in church at Spring Ridge First Church of God when I had a kidney stone attack. I had already had two kidney stones surgically removed, so I knew immediately what it was. I told my wife, Mary Ellen and we immediately go up and went to the hospital. When we got to the hospital, they x-rayed me and the stone was lodged between the kidney and the bladder. They gave me pain medication and inserted a catheter into my bladder. The next morning they prepped me for surgery. The last thing I remember as I was being wheeled into the surgery room, was Brother Luther Moore holding my hand and praying for me. For some reason they decided to x-ray me in the operating room to see if the stone had moved one way or the other. Guess what? I did not have a kidney stone in the left side of my body. Remember, I had a catheter in my bladder, so I could not have passed a stone as large as it was. Besides, there was a strainer in the line going into the jug.

Now, do you think I should care about "how" God removed the stone, or do you think I should care about "why" God removed the stone? Yes, I am proud to proclaim that I am a recipient of the "mysterious" miracle healing power of "The Almighty God". Amen!

It is not "how" God does something, but the "why" He does it that really matters.

John was told to take the scroll and eat it, and it will taste sweet in his mouth, but it will sour his stomach. The eating of this scroll probably refers to the ingesting of the Holy Word of God; to partake of His promises and to also be mindful of the judgements that He is going to send on the world. The sweetness in his mouth represents God's "Amazing Grace" and the sourness represents the judgements that He is going to send on this evil world.

Ezekiel received a similar command: **Ezekiel 3:1 – 4** (1) And he said to me, "Son of man, eat what is before you, eat this scroll; then go and speak to the house of Israel." (2) So I opened my mouth and he gave me the scroll to eat. (3) The he said to me, "Son of man, eat this scroll I am giving you and fill your stomach with it." So I ate it, and it tasted as sweet as honey in my mouth. (4) He then said to me, "Son of man, go now to the house of Israel and speak my words to them."

Just as Ezekiel was told to speak to the house of Israel, John was told by the mighty angel that he must prophesy again to the many peoples, languages, nations and kings. Everyone must hear the word of God preached.

The symbolism of John eating the scroll extends to all others who need to partake of the word of God. Though there will be brightness and pain at times in our lives, the ultimate glory of God will be the prize collected by all of those who put their Lord and Savior first.

John was also reassured that his exile to the Isle of Patmos was not permanent and that he was destined to witness to many people. It seems that God always has every "i" dotted and every "t" crossed in the plan for our lives when we let Him lead and we follow and do His will.

Chapter 5 – Revelation Chapter 11 – the Ending

Revelation 11:1 – 14 The two witnesses. (1) I was given a reed like a measuring rod and was told, "Go and measure the temple of God and the alter and count the worshipers there. (2) But exclude the outer court, do not measure it, because it has been given to the Gentiles. They will trample on the Holy City for forty-two months. (3) And I will give power to my two witnesses, and they will prophesy for 1260 days clothed in sack cloth. (4) These are the two olive trees and the two lampstands that stand before the Lord of the earth. (5) If anyone tries to harm them, fire comes from their mouths and devours their enemies. This is how anyone who wants to harm them must die. (6) These men have the power to shut up the sky, so that it will not rain during the time that they are prophesying; and, they have the power to turn the water into blood, and to strike the earth with every kind of plague that they want, as often as they want. (7) Now when they have finished their testimony, the beast that comes up from the Abyss will attack them and overpower and kill them. (8) Their bodies will lie in the street of the great city, which is figuratively called Sodom and Egypt, where also their Lord was crucified. (9) For three and a half days, men from every people, tribe, language and nation will gaze on their bodies and refuse them burial. (10) The inhabitants of the earth will gloat over them and will celebrate by sending each other gifts, because these two prophets had tormented those who live on the earth. (11) But, after three and a half days, a breath of life from God entered them and they stood on their feet and terror struck those who saw them. (12) Then they heard a loud voice from Heaven saying to them, "Come up here." And they went up into Heaven in a cloud, while their enemies looked on. (13) At that very hour there was a severe earthquake and a tenth of the city collapsed; seven thousand people were killed in the earthquake, and the survivors were terrified and gave glory to the God of Heaven. (14) The second woe has passed; and, the third woe is coming soon.

This is my favorite passage in Revelation. It depicts the accuracy and the literal fulfillment of the prophecies of Revelation.

In **Revelation 10:1 – 11** John was told that this was a direct revelation from God and he must testify to all people about it.

There is no explanation of the command given to John to measure the temple. During the last three and a half years, forty two months or 1260 days (which is the exact same time frame in the Grecian calendar) of the Tribulation period, the temple has already been desecrated, the holy sacrifices have been stopped and the worship of the world ruler has been installed.

Daniel 9:27 He will confirm a covenant with many for one seven. In the middle of the seven, he will put an end to sacrifice and offering. And on a wing of the temple he will set up an abomination that causes desolation, until the end that is decreed is poured out on him.

Daniel is speaking about the antichrist or the world ruler who will make a covenant with Israel for seven years. The first half of the seven years will be relatively peaceful. The last three and a half years, he will break the covenant and will establish his rule and authority over the people. This last three and a half years, 42 months, or 1260days is called the Great Tribulation because of all of the turmoil and unrest of the world. This is when God will send most of His judgements on the world.

According to scripture, Jerusalem, the Holy City, will be trampled by the Gentiles for the final forty two months before the second coming of Jesus. Since about 600 BC, Israel has never been in full possession of their holy places except by Gentile tolerance and permission. This is still true today, without the support of the United States, Israel could not retain its independence. There has been short periods of time when Israel temporarily retained control of their holy places, but it will never be permanent until the second coming of Christ.

These two witnesses will be prophets in the end time. Their prophecy will be during the same time that the world rulers will possess the temple and turn it into a religious center for the worship of himself.

There is a major difference between religion and Christianity. Religion is humans trying to work their way to their God. Christianity is God coming to men and women through a relationship with Jesus Christ.

John 3:16 For God so loved the world that He gave his only begotten Son that whosoever believeth in Him shall not perish but have ever lasting life.

John 14:6 Jesus said, "I am the way, the truth and the life, no one comes to the Father except through me."

This is the salvation plan wrapped up in two verses. Everything else that we do as Christians just puts stars in our crowns. But you cannot believe in Jesus if you do not live the life that He has planned for us. You cannot give Him lip service. If you talk the walk, you must walk the talk.

These two witnesses are what I call "Power Packed Witnesses". They have the almighty power of God at their disposal to do whatever they deem necessary to witness to the hard headed people. They will get some of the people's attention when fire starts coming out of their mouth devouring people. They may be hard headed, but this will be an attention getter for some.

The reference to the two olive trees and the two lampstands is this. The olive tree represents peace, when you offer peace to someone, you are said to have extended an olive branch to them. The lampstands give off the light. When you are plugged into the word of God, you can see your way through a dark and evil world. These two witnesses will offer God's peace and amazing grace to a dark and evil world. Those who receive the word will be saved.

The emergence of these two witnesses during the Great Tribulation presents a big problem for the leaders of the one world government. They cannot be killed, and they have the power of Elijah and some of the other prophets. They also have the power to strike the world with plagues, just as Moses did the Egyptians.

Now comes the meat of what Revelation is all about. You will see how and why the prophecies of Revelation will be literally fulfilled. These are not symbolic prophecies; they will be fulfilled.

When the testimony of these two witnesses is finished, they will be attacked, overpowered and killed. They will lie in the street where they were killed for three and a half days. All of the world will see them lying there and no one will come to bury them. After three and a half days, a breath of life from God will enter them and they will stand on their feet. A loud voice from Heaven will say to them, "Come up here." They will rise and go up into Heaven with the whole world being able to watch them ascend into Heaven, and terror will strike all of those who see them rise and go up into Heaven.

Before December 17, 1974, the literal fulfillment of this prophecy was not possible. On this date, the first communication satellite was launched into orbit. Since then, we have been able to see things around the world at the same time that they are happening.

Now when John wrote this he had no idea of how this would be accomplished. It has taken men two thousand years for mankind to figure out how to build satellites and televisions. This is the only way that people around the world will be able to witness this event as it takes place.

Do you think that this may be a very important milestone in the timetable for the future of this world in God's plan? This should be enough evidence to convince anyone that these prophecies will be fulfilled and that they may be closer to being fulfilled than we think.

Even though God is allowing the terrible events of the Great Tribulation to take place, it is also evident that God is still in control and that He can provide testimony of His power and His grace even under these terrible circumstances.

Revelation 11:15 – 19 The Seventh Trumpet and the third woe. (15)
The seventh angel sounded his trumpet, and there were loud voices
in Heaven which said, "The kingdom of the world has become the
kingdom of our Lord and His Christ, and He will reign forever and
ever." (16) And the twenty-four elders who were seated on their
thrones before God, fell on their faces and worshiped God saying: (17)
"We give thanks to you, Lord God Almighty. The one who is and who
was because you have taken your great Power and have begun to
reign. (18) The nations were angry, and your wrath has come. The time
has come for judging the dead, and for rewarding your servants, the
prophets and your saints, and those who reverence your name, both
great and small and for destroying those who destroy the earth." (19)
Then God's temple in Heaven was opened and within His temple was
seen the ark of His covenant; and there came flashes of lightening,
rumblings, peals of thunder, and earthquake and a great hailstorm.

Earthly rulers have only temporary power. Evil in this world is only temporary. God has sovereign authority. His power is almighty and eternal, and His victory is everlasting. This means that suffering and persecution of Christians is only temporary. God will judge evil, and He will reward faithfulness, and he will rule the world forever.

Overall, this eleventh chapter may be the most important in all of Revelation. Until the invention of satellite television, there was no way that people thought that this prophecy could be anything more than a symbolic prophecy. This is one of the greatest proofs in the Bible that these prophecies can and will be fulfilled literally.

Now can you believe that God was scrolling this across the sky for John to see. Remember that he says sixty nine times that he sees, or he saw, or he has seen.

Revelation 12:1 – 17 The woman and the Dragon. (1) A great and wondrous sign appeared in the Heaven, a woman clothed with the sun, and the moon under her feet, and a crown of twelve stars on her head. (2) She was pregnant and cried out in pain as she was about to give birth. (3) Then another sign appeared in Heaven; an enormous red dragon with seven heads and ten horns and seven crowns on his heads. (4) His tail swept a third of the stars out of the sky and flung them to the earth. The dragon stood in front of the woman who was about to give birth, so that he might devour her child the moment it was born. (5) She gave birth to a son, a male child, who will rule all the nations with an iron scepter. And her child was snatched up to God and His throne. (6) The woman fled into the desert to a place prepared for her by God, where she might be taken care of for 1260 days. (7) And there was war in Heaven. Michael and his angels fought against the dragon, and the dragon and his angels fought back. (8) But he was not strong enough and they lost their place in Heaven. (9) The great dragon was hurled down, that ancient serpent, called the devil or Satan, who leads the whole world astray. He was hurled down to the earth and his angels with him. (10) Then I heard a loud voice in Heaven say: "Now have come the salvation and the power and the kingdom of our God and the authority of His Christ. For the accuser of our brothers, who accuses them before our God day and night, has been hurled down. (11) They overcame him by the Blood of the Lamb and by the word of their testimony; they did not love their lives so much as to shrink form death. (12) "Therefore, rejoice you Heavens and you who dwell in them! But woe, to the earth and the sea, because the devil has gone down to you! He is filled with fury, because he knows that his time is short." (13) When the dragon saw that he had been hurled down to the earth, he pursued the woman who had given birth to the male child. (14) The woman was given the two wings of a great eagle, so that she might fly to the place that was prepared for her in the desert, where she would be taken care of for a time, times, and a halftime, out of the serpents reach. (15) Then from his mouth, the serpent spewed water like a river to overtake the woman and sweep her away with the torrent. (16) But the earth helped the woman by opening up its mouth and swallowing the river that the dragon had spewed out of his mouth. (17) Then the dragon was enraged at the woman and went off to make war against the rest of her offspring; those who obey God's commandments and hold to the testimony of Jesus. And the dragon stood on the shore of the sea.

Jesus was born of woman, suffered, died and was raised, and ascended to Heaven. Satan, the dragon, lost the heavenly battle and was cast down from Heaven to earth. Jesus' victory is sure. He still reigns in Heaven. Christians must still endure suffering because Satan is still loose on earth and enraged against the followers of Christ because he knows his time is short.

In the redemption of the Blood of Jesus on the cross, came the power for Christians to overcome Satan and to establish God's eternal kingdom life for His people under the authority of Jesus Christ. God's people can overcome the devil through the atoning death of Jesus on the cross. The blood that He shed paid the ultimate price for our sins to be forgiven. Even Satan recognizes the power and authority of God.

In the face of the coming end of history of the world as we know it, God's people are called to a higher commitment of obedience. Only the obedient will be able to stand against the evil dragon Satan. Those who stand for Christ and bear a strong testimony will be persecuted by this world, yet, the Lord promises victory to His people.

We see this persecution beginning to be more prevalent in the world today than ever before. The number one priority of the world media today is to ridicule Christians. If you are a Christian and stand up for morals and values taught in the Bible, you will be ridiculed and avoided like someone with a plague. But, take heart, you will receive the prize of the victor. The world will receive its coming judgement and justice.

There are seven important personages represented in Revelation chapters twelve through fourteen:

1) The woman represents the nation of Israel. **Revelation 12:1 – 15**
2) The dragon or devil, represents Satan. **Revelation 12:7 – 17, 13:1 – 2, 4 and 11**
3) The man child is Jesus Christ. **Revelation 12:4 – 16**
4) Michael represents all of the heavenly angels. **Revelation 12:7 – 9**
5) The remnant of Israel is represented by the 144,000. **Revelation 7:4 – 8, 14:1 – 5**
6) The beast out of the sea is the world leader of the end time. **Revelation 13:1 – 8**
7) The beast out of the earth is a religious leader who is the false prophet that supports the world dictator. **Revelation 12:11 – 17**

The sun and the moon in verse one is representative of Jacob and Rachel, the forbearers of the twelve tribes of the nation of Israel. Jacob had six sons by Leah and two by her maidservant, Zilpah. He also had two by Rachel, which were Joseph and Benjamin and two more by her maidservant Bilpah. This gave Joseph a total of twelve sons who would become the fathers of the twelve tribes of Israel. The twelve tribes are represented by the crown on the woman's head with the twelve stars in it.

The fact that the woman is pregnant and in pain refers to the experience and suffering of the nation of Israel down through the centuries while waiting for the coming of her messiah. Her suffering refers to the nation of Israel as a whole, and not to Mary, the mother of Jesus.

The enormous red dragon with the seven heads, ten horns and seven crowns on his head refers to the Roman Empire.

Daniel 7:7 "After that, in my vision at night, I looked and there before me was a fourth beast, terrifying, frightening and very powerful. It had large iron teeth; it crushed and devoured its victims and trampled underfoot whatever was left. It was different from all of the former beasts and it had ten horns."

This dragon may also refer to the power of the Roman Empire during the life of Jesus. The dragon is pictured as waiting for the birth of the man child to devour it as soon as it is born. King Herod wanted to kill Jesus when He was just a baby.

The child is described as the one, who will rule all nations with an iron scepter. This will be fulfilled in the millennial kingdom when Jesus Christ rules the world. This was predicted in Psalm 2 9 "You will rule them with and iron scepter; you will dash them to pieces like pottery.

The statement that the child will be "snatched up to God and to His throne" refers to the ascension of Christ to Heaven after His resurrection and after He had told His disciples that He would send the Holy Spirit to dwell in them, and that they would witness to all of the world.

The woman being put in a place where she will be protected by God for 1260 days is the nation of Israel being protected through the Great Tribulation. The 1260 days, 42 months, or three and a half years will be the exact length of time of the Great Tribulation before Christ comes the second time to claim His kingdom. God can count!

Jeremiah 30:7 "How awful that day will be; none will be like it! It will be a time of trouble for Jacob, but he will be saved out of it."

Though many in Israel will perish, God will save a remnant as He has done down through the ages and they will be "His people".

Zachariah 13:8 – 9 In the whole land, declares the Lord, two thirds will be struck down, yet, one third will be left in it. This one third, I, will bring into the fire; I will refine them like silver, and test them like gold. They will call on My name, and I will answer them; I will say "They are my people", and they will say "The Lord is our God".

The nation of Israel will be rescued by Christ when He returns again. **Romans 11:25 – 29** [(25)] I do not want you to be ignorant of this mystery, brothers, so that you may not be conceited: Israel has experienced a hardening in part until the full number of Gentiles has come in. (26) And so, all Israel will be saved, as it is written: The deliverer will come from Zion, He will turn godlessness away from Jacob. (27) And this is my covenant with them when I take away their sins. (28) As far as the gospel is concerned, they are enemies, on your account, but as far as election is concerned, they are loved on account of the Patriarchs. (29) For God's gifts and His call are irrevocable.

The Jewish people as a whole may not yet believe that Jesus Christ came as their Lord and Savior, but when Jesus returns those that accept Him will be shown the same mercy and grace as we Gentiles were. Those will be the people who will be the chosen ones as God's remnant to fulfill the scriptures.

God fore knew Israel; what she was, what she would do, and what she would ultimately become. He has not rejected Israel and He is not through with her. Rather, He has broadened the focus of His grace and has brought the Gentiles into His covenant. Through His sovereign grace, He is extending His mercy still today, by offering salvation to all people.

Paul is saying here that the nation of Israel will be saved in the end time. Jerusalem is called the Holy City throughout the Bible. Remember it is mentioned 888 times in the Bible. Why should the nation of Israel be forced to give up any part of this city? Especially to the Palestinians who have tried to destroy the whole nation of Israel for thousands of years.

Revelation 12:7 – 9 is a very hard passage for limp wristed people who believe that God is only a God of love, and that if we just love everybody and do not stand up for God's principles and morals, everything will be alright. God has always been at war with Satan, and always will be until Satan is defeated and thrown into the lake of fire, along with the beast and the false prophet, where they will be tormented day and night forever and ever. Satan being cast down to the earth marks the beginning of the most awful of time in the history of the world, the Great Tribulation.

Now that Satan has been kicked out of heaven, he will focus his full fury on the earth. He is filled with fury because he knows his time is short. He knows prophecy, and he understands that his time is limited. The only way to overcome him is by "the Blood of the Lamb"; by faithful witness for God and being willing to suffer and die if necessary.

Salvation comes with a price and with salvation comes power to overcome. We must stand up for what the Bible teaches us. We cannot be two parts to make a whole. We cannot take the ways of the world and relate them to a right relationship with God. You cannot serve two masters.

The woman "the nation of Israel", will be protected by God during the Great Tribulation. There will be great suffering and many will die, but God will save a remnant of Israel as He has done many times in the past.

The term time, times, and a halftime is 1 year, 2 years, and a half year, making it the three and a half years, 42 months, or 1260 days.

John saw the devil spewing a river of filth out of his mouth to overtake the woman. The power of Satan during this time will be tremendous, but the power given to the believer through the "Blood of the Lamb" will be even more powerful and will sustain them. Even though they perish, they will have everlasting life. There is no power greater than the power of the Blood of Jesus Christ.

Revelation 13:1 – 10 The Beast out of the Sea. (1) And I saw a beast coming up out of the sea. He had ten horns and seven heads, with ten crowns on his horns and on each head a blasphemous name. (2) The beast resembled a leopard, but had feet like those of a bear, and a mouth like that of a lion. The dragon gave the beast his power, and his throne, and great authority. (3) One of the heads of the beast seemed to have a fatal wound, but the fatal wound had healed. The whole world was astonished and followed the beast. (4) Men worshiped the dragon, because he had given authority to the beast, and they also worshipped the beast, and asked, "Who is like the beast? Who can make war against him?" (5) The beast was given a mouth to utter proud words and blasphemies and to exercise his authority for forty two months. (6) He opened his mouth to blaspheme God and to slander His name, and His dwelling place and those who lived in Heaven. (7) He was given power to make war against the Saints and to conquer them. And he was given authority over every tribe, people, language, and nation. (8) All inhabitants of the earth will worship the beast; all whose names have not been written in the Book of Life, belonging to the Lamb that was slain from the creation of the world. (9) He who has an ear, let him hear. If anyone is to go into captivity, into captivity he will go. (10) If anyone is to be killed with the sword, with the sword he will be killed. This calls for patient endurance and faithfulness on the part of the Saints.

Satan often works through human rulers who have great authority, who boast of great pride, and say, "look at me, see how powerful I am, how great I am, and they even claim to be God." To worship such human authorities, whether it is politically or religiously, is to worship Satan and have eternal damnation in Hell.

The beast out of the sea is often identified as the antichrist or the man of lawlessness.

I John 2:18 – 19 (18) "Dear children, this is the last hour; and as you have heard the antichrist is coming, even now many antichrist has come. This is how we know that it is the last hour. (19) They went out from us, but they did not really belong to us. For if they had really belonged to us, they would have remained with us; but their going showed that none of them belonged to us."

2 John 1:7 – 11 (7) Many deceivers, who do not acknowledge Jesus Christ as coming in the flesh have gone out into the world. Any such person is the deceiver and the antichrist. (8) Watch out that you do not lose what you have worked for, but that you may be rewarded fully. (9) Anyone who runs ahead and does not continue in the teaching of Christ, does not have God; whoever continues in the teaching has both Father and Son. (10) If anyone comes to you and does not bring this teaching, do not take him into your house or welcome him. (11) Anyone who welcomes him shares in his wicked work.

What John is saying here is that we as Christians are going to get lambasted from all sides with the filth and the evil of the world. Some of it is even going to come out of the pulpits and classrooms of our churches. The greatest threat that we Christians have is, we get beat over the head with this filth and evil so much that we become tolerant of it. Two of the greatest examples of this is abortion and homosexuality. If homosexuality was evil and a sin from Genesis chapter nineteen through Revelation, it is still evil and a sin today.

Abortion is so evil that no one had even thought of it from the writings of the Old Testament through the New Testament. It took an evil world to concoct the belief that a thing growing inside of a woman's womb was a fetus and not a baby. If a fetus does not have life, how does it grow? Why does it have fingers, toes, hands, feet, a mouth, eyes, a nose a heart and all the other parts that make up our body?

If President Barack Obama does not know when life begins, I can enlighten him: at conception. Dead things do not grow. Try planting a dead seed or a dead stick and see how much fruit you get.

2 Thessalonians 2:3 – 4 (3) Do not let anyone conceive you in any way! For that day will not come until the rebellion occurs and the man of lawlessness is revealed, the man doomed to destruction. (4) He will oppose and exalt himself over everything that is called God, or is worshipped, so that he sets himself up in God's temple, proclaiming himself to be God.

God allows the evil forces of Satan to exercise control and inflict punishment, but their time of power has been limited by Him long before they even gain power. Satan does not control time and eternity. God controls time and eternity.

The sacrificial death of Jesus on the cross was part of God's magnificent eternal plan to create His own faithful people who would not worship Satan.

The antichrist will convince the world that he can end all wars. He will pose as a savior to world economies. He will promise to end religious differences through a one world church. He will be a smooth talker who will convince the people that he can solve all the world's problems. Does sound like our politicians of today? There will be just enough religion nixed with their hunger for power to be able to convince the people that they will be their savior.

There are many religions in this world. Many people worship many Gods even ones that they make with their own hands. John 3:16

and John 14:6 are the key verses in the Bible that reveal God's plan of salvation for His elect people: Christians.

If you have not accepted Jesus Christ as your Lord and Savior, you are hell bound. Nothing but the shed blood of Jesus will wash away your sins and give you eternal life. You do have a choice: Heaven or Hell, Christianity or religion.

The sea in this passage represents the Mediterranean area, which is where the beast, where the future world leader will come from. This area contains a majority of the oil in the world and they will have the money and the power to control the rest of the world.

The ten horns represent ten governments that have banded together for more power. The crowns are diadems of emblems of their governmental authority. Their blasphemous names indicate that they are opposed to God. The seven heads are a select group of leaders within this system that will be calling the shots. They will be in total control.

Daniel saw four beasts in his dream that represented world power by authoritarian rule. Three of the four have been fulfilled, and the fourth one will be the antichrist.

Daniel 7:4 "The first one was like a lion, and it had the wings of an eagle. I watched until its wings were torn off and it was lifted from the ground so that it stood on its two feet like a man, and was given the heart of a man."

This was the Babylonian Empire. They had the power of a lion, the king of the beasts, and the ability of the eagle, the king of the birds. This gave them the ability to see everything and to strike quickly with deadly force. The heart of a man being given to the beast refers to **Daniel 4:28 – 37**. When God allowed Nebuchadnezzar's dream to come true that his kingdom would be taken from him and he would eat grass like an animal.

In verses thirty four through thirty eight, Nebuchadnezzar recognizes that God is in command of all things at all times. He raised his eyes towards Heaven and his sanity and his kingdom were restored to him.

Daniel 4:37 Now I , Nebuchadnezzar, praise and exalt and glorify the king of heaven, because everything He does is right, and all His ways are just. And those who walk in pride, He is able to humble.

Daniel 7:5 And there before me was a second beast, which looked like a bear. It was raised up on one of its sides, and it had three ribs in its mouth between its teeth. It was told, "Get up and eat your fill of flesh."

This second kingdom was the Medo-Persian Empire that conquered Babylon. It had great power like a bear, but it lacked the charisma and the royalty of the Babylonians. The bear being raised up on one of its sides indicates that the Persians had greater power than the Medes. The three ribs in its mouth probably represent the three provinces of Babylonia, Persia and Medo.

Daniel 7:6 After that I looked and there beside me was another beast, one that looked like a leopard. And on its back it had four wings like that of a bird. This beast had four heads and it was given authority to rule.

The leopard represents the Greek Empire and the rapid conquests of Alexander the Great. Alexander used great speed to capture all of western Asia. He moved from province to province so fast the people did not have time to prepare a defense. When he died, his kingdom was divided among his four generals represented by the four heads and four wings.

Now this is where the rubber begins to meet the road. Daniel sees the same things happening that John sees while he is exiled on the Isle of Patmos. Remember in the Bible, in the time of Daniel and John, it took two witnesses to an event to confirm that it was a truth. With Daniel and John seeing the same things, it must be accepted as the truth.

Daniel saw this happening in a dream which he did not understand. The dream was interpreted by an angel or one of the Saints that was in Heaven near the throne of God.

John had a better view. He was sitting on the Isle of Patmos all by himself. He witnessed these future events taking place as God scrolled them across the sky on His big screen television. You say God did not have a big screen television. Remember this is the same God who parted the Red Sea for the Israelites to escape from Egypt. This is the same God that stopped the Jordan River from flowing during flood stage so the Israelites could cross the Jordan into the Promised Land.

This story if found in **Joshua 3: – 17** and God used this event to reemphasize to the Israelites, after wandering around in the desert for forty years, that He was still in charge. How much confidence in God do you think the Israelites gained while they were walking across the Jordan River and on the up side the river was piling up and where they were walking, the riverbed was dry? This is the power of the Almighty God that we serve.

Daniel 7:7 – 8 (7) After that in my vision at night, I looked and there before me was a fourth beast: terrifying and very powerful. It had large iron teeth, it crushed and devoured its victims and trampled underfoot what was left. It was different from all the former beasts and it had ten horns. (8) While I was thinking about the horns, there was another horn, a little one, which came up among them, and three of the horns were uprooted before it. This horn had eyes like the eyes of a man and a mouth that spoke boastfully.

This will be a future empire that is setup to control the world after the Rapture of all Christians. The world will be void of the power of God and the entire world will be controlled by this empire.

Daniel 7:9 – 10 (9) As I looked, thrones were set in place and the Ancient of Days took His seat. His clothing was as white as snow, (pure and clean), the hair of His head was white like wool. His throne was flaming with fire and its wheels were all ablaze. (10) A river of fire was flowing, coming out from before Him. Thousands upon thousands attended Him. Ten thousand times ten thousand stood before Him. The court was set and the books were opened.

This is in reference to the Second Coming of Jesus. These are the exact same numbers that John saw in **Revelation 5:11**. Then I looked and heard the voices of many angels, numbering thousands upon thousands and ten thousand time ten thousand, (100,000,000). This will be the largest choir ever assembled.

Daniel 7:11 Then I continued to watch because of the boastful words the horn was speaking. I kept looking until the beast was slain and its body was destroyed and thrown into the blazing river.

Revelation 19: 20 But, the beast was captured and with him the false prophet, who had performed the miraculous signs on his behalf. With these signs, he had deluded those who had received the mark of the beast and worshipped its image. The two of them were thrown alive into the fiery lake of burning sulfur.

Is this a coincidence that these two verses parallel one another so closely, even though they were written hundreds of years apart?

Daniel 7:12 The other beasts had been stripped of their authority, but were allowed to live for a period of time.

This most likely refers back to the Babylonian, Medo-Persian, and the Greek empires, which were allowed to flourish and control much of the world as it was then before being destroyed.

Refer back to **Daniel 7:10** where the court was seated and the books were opened, and we will fast forward to **Daniel 12:1 – 4** (1) "At that time, Michael, the great prince who protects your people will arise. There will be a time of great distress such as has not happened from the beginnings of nations until then. But at that time, your people, everyone whose name is found written in the book, will be delivered. (2) Multitudes who sleep in the dust of the earth will awake, some to everlasting life, others to everlasting shame and contempt. (3) Those who are wise will shine like the brightness of the Heavens, and those who lead many others to righteousness will shine like the stars forever and ever. (4) But you, Daniel, close up and seal the words of the scroll, until the end of time. Many will go here and there to increase knowledge."

Was this the same scroll that John saw being unsealed and rolled out in Heaven, or was it another scroll? You be the judge, I am not sure. But it really does not matter because both of them were witnesses to the end of time as we know it.

Daniel 7:13 – 14 (13) In my vision at night, I looked and there before me was one like a son of man, coming with the clouds of Heaven. He approached the Ancient of Days and was led into His presence. (14) He was given authority, glory and sovereign power; all peoples, nations and men of every nation worshipped Him. His kingdom is an everlasting dominion that will not pass away, and His kingdom is one that will never be destroyed.

Revelation 5:13 Then I heard every creature in Heaven and on earth and under the earth and on the sea, and all that is in them, saying; "To Him who sits on the throne, and to the Lamb, be praise and honor, and glory and power, forever and ever."

God's Saints will inherit His kingdom and will possess it for eternity. The Saints are the people of God. You do not have to have people to vote on you after you are dead to become a Saint. Saint means on set apart for God's service. The word Saint does not indicate sinlessness. All the Saints of God, the people He has elected to do His will, will receive eternal life. Some will receive more crowns because of their dedicated service to God. Some will smell like smoke when they get to Heaven, just escaping the gates of Hell.

Daniel 7:15 – 28 The Interpretation of the Dream. (15)I, Daniel, was troubled in spirit, and the visions that passed through my mind disturbed me. (16) I approached one of those standing there and asked him the true meaning of all of this. So he told me and gave me the interpretations of those things: (17) The four great beasts are four kingdoms that will rise from the earth. (18) But, the Saints of the Most High will receive the kingdom and will possess it forever – yes, forever and ever. (19) Then I wanted to know the true meaning of the fourth beast, which was different from all of the others and the most terrifying, with its iron teeth and bronze claws – the beast that crushed and devoured its victims and trampled underfoot whatever was left. (20) I also wanted to know about the ten horns on its head, and about the other one that came up before which three of them fell – the horn that looked more opposing than the others and that had eyes and a mouth that spoke boastfully. (21) As I watched, this horn was waging war against the Saints, and defeating them, (22) until the Ancient of Days came and pronounced judgement in favor of the Saints of the Most High, and the time came when they possessed the kingdom. (23) He gave this explanation; the fourth beast is the fourth kingdom that will appear on earth. It will be different from all the other kingdoms, and will devour the whole earth, trampling it down and crushing it. (24) The ten horns are ten kings who will come from this kingdom. After this another king will arise, different from the earlier ones; he will subdue three kings. (25) He will speak against the Most High and oppress His Saints, and try to change the set times and the laws. The Saints will be handed over to him for a time, times and a half time (three and a half years – the last half of the Tribulation which is called the Great Tribulation because of its severity and the awful things that will take place during this time period). (26) But, the court will sit and his power will be taken away and completely destroyed forever. (27) Then, the sovereignty, power and greatness of the kingdoms under the whole Heaven will be handed over to the Saints, the people of the Most High. His kingdom will be everlasting, and all rulers will worship and obey Him. (28) This is the end of the matter! I, Daniel, was deeply troubled by my thoughts and my face turned pale, and I kept the matter to myself.

The similarities of what Daniel saw in his dream and what John saw while on the Isle of Patmos, is shockingly the same. The first three beasts and their kingdoms have been fulfilled and the one still to come is worse than all the others combined.

Revelation 13:9 is the same command that was given to the seven churches, which means, if you hear the word, you had better heed the word. This emphasizes the sovereignty of God, which takes into consideration the response of all people who hear the Gospel message.

Revelation 13:10 states that some will be captured and that some will be killed. But, all who remain faithful and endure will receive salvation from God. They may be persecuted and die, but they will receive their eternal blessings from God. On the other hand, those who are wicked and deserve punishment will receive it in this time or in eternity. You will be weighed in the scales of life. Don't come up lacking on the short side.

Revelation 13:11 – 18 The Beast out of the Land. (11) Then I saw another beast coming out of the earth. He had two horns like a lamb, but he spoke like a dragon. (12) He exercised all the authority of the first beast on his behalf and made the earth and its inhabitants worship the first beast, whose fatal wound had been healed. (13) And he performed great and miraculous signs, even causing fire to come down from heaven to earth in full view of men. (14) Because of the signs, he was given power to do on behalf of the first beast, he deceived the inhabitants of the earth. He ordered them to set up an image of the beast who was wounded and yet lived. (15) He was given power to give breath to the image of the first beast, so that it could speak and cause all who worshiped the image to be killed. [16] He also forced everyone small and great, rich and poor, free and slave to receive a mark on his right hand or on his forehead, [17] so that no one could buy or sell unless he had the mark, which is the name of the number of the beast. [18] This calls for wisdom!! If anyone has insight let him calculate the number of the beast, for it is man's number. "His number is 666."

The fact that this beast comes out of the earth refers to him coming out of the world, not simply the land of Palestine. The instantaneous communication around the world and the ability to travel faster than sound from city to city gives much credence to this possibility.

The two horns indicate that he had some power and authority as a political leader. He was also pictured as having the two horns like a lamb which points to him as having religious (not Christian) characteristics, which is supported by the fact in **Revelation 19:20,** he is called a false prophet. It is probable that he is a Gentile who supports the world ruler and uses his power to cause many people to worship the world ruler.

As a false prophet, he was able to provide some basis for the belief in the beast out of the sea, by the miracles that he performed. The image of the beast that he sets up is referred to several times in this chapter and six more times in Revelation. Because of the fire that comes down from Heaven, he probably compared himself to having the same power of Elijah when he called fire down from Heaven to destroy the messengers of King Ahaziah.

2 Kings 1:9 – 12 [9] Then he sent to Elijah a captain with his fifty men. The captain went up to Elijah and said to him, "Man of God, the king says, come down." [10] Elijah answered the captain, "If I am a man of God, may fire come down from Heaven and consume you and your fifty men." Then fire came down from Heaven and consumed the captain and his men. [11] At this time the king sent another captain to Elijah with his fifty men. The captain said to him, "Man of God, this is what the king says, Come down at once." [12] "If I am a man of God," Elijah replied, "may fire come down from Heaven and consume you and your fifty men." Then fire came down from Heaven and consumed him and his fifty men.

If this false prophet has this kind of power, he will be able to scare and deceive many people. He was able to contrive, supernaturally or naturally, that he had given breath to the image and that it was alive and breathing. This will cause many people to worship the beast, and if they do not, they will be killed.

This mark will probably be accomplished by inserting a computer chip of some kind under the skin. This method is used today to track the movement of all kinds of animals and it would certainly be possible for a one world government to accomplish this. Who would stop them? Remember, all Christians have been "Raptured", and the world is void of the presence of God.

The number 7 represents perfection or completion in the Bible. The number 6 may mean that this was as close as the antichrist could get to have people believe that he was now their God. The number "666" probably represents the antichrist, the false prophet and Satan. This is the satanic Trinitarian who will be in power at this time.

The world ruler will actually for a short time, rule over the entire world, and the beast out of the earth will support him and cause people to worship him. The evil in men's hearts will be allowed its full manifestation, but then it will be subjected to the judgement of God at the second coming of Jesus.

This is what Jesus says about Himself and what He says about the antichrist who is to come.

John 5:37 – 40 Testimonies about Jesus. (37) And the Father who has sent me, Himself, testified concerning me. You have never heard His voice nor seen His form, (38) nor does His word dwell in you, for you do not believe the one He sent. (39) You diligently study the scriptures, because you think that by them you possess eternal life. These scriptures testify about me. (40) Yet you refuse to come to me to have eternal life.

This is Jesus chastising the Jewish religious leaders after they condemned Him and persecuted Him for healing the crippled man by the pool of Bethesda on the Sabbath Day. They did not care that the man was healed, they were concerned only that one of their rules had been broken.

John 5:41 – 43 (41) I do not accept praise from men, (42) but I know you. I know that you do not have the love of God in your hearts. (43) I have come in my Father's name and you do not accept me; but if someone else comes in his own name, you will accept him.

Jesus is warning the world of the coming of the antichrist. Jesus is the greatest revelation of God revealed in the scriptures and manifested in the flesh. Some of these Jewish religious leaders claimed to seek God, but they refused to seek and follow Jesus. Diligent study of the scriptures is fruitless if it does not lead to faith in Jesus as our Lord and Savior. Faith not facts is the ultimate purpose of scripture study.

The Jewish leaders read Moses' laws and teachings to determine rules for living and judging others. But they refused to believe that Jesus was the Son of God even though they witnessed many miracles that He did while healing the sick, the blind, and the lame.

John 5:44 – 46 (44) How can you believe if you accept praise from one another, yet you make no effort to obtain praise that comes from the only God. (45) But do not think that I will be your accuser before the Father. Your accuser is Moses, on whom your hopes are set. (46) If you believed in Moses, you would believe in Me, for he wrote about Me.

The whole purpose of the Bible from Genesis through Revelation is to convince people that Jesus is the "Son of God", the Lamb of God, and the Lion of Judah. He is the love and compassion of God, but He is also the administrator of justice and righteousness.

A well known evangelist named Charles "Chuck" Colson was being interviewed by Larry King on the CNN television network. The main topic of the interview was why people believe in Jesus Christ as their Lord and Savior. After the interview was over, Larry King asked Chuck Colson if he could convince him why he should become a believer. Chuck Colson told him that if he would have dinner with him and give him two hours that he could. At the end of the two hours, Larry King looked at him and said, "You have not convinced me that I need to become a believer." Chuck Colson looked at him and said, "Larry it is because you do not want to believe."

This will be the mindset of everyone left on the earth after the Rapture of all Christians. There are many good people today who do good things for others, but they have not accepted Jesus Christ as their Lord and Savior. Good deeds or riches will not save anyone from Hell!

Revelation 14:1 – 5 The Lamb and the 144,000. (1) Then I looked, and there before me was the Lamb, standing on Mount Zion, and with Him, 144,000 who had His name and His Father's name written on their foreheads. (2) And I heard a sound from Heaven like the roar of rushing waters and like a loud peal of thunder. The sound that I heard was like that of harpists playing their harps. (3) And they sang a new song before the throne and before the four living creatures and before the elders. No one could learn the song except the 14,000, who had been redeemed from the earth. (4) These are those who did not defile themselves with women, for they kept themselves pure. They follow the Lamb wherever he goes. They were purchased from among men and offered as first fruits to God and to the Lamb. (5) No lie was found in their mouths, they are blameless.

Revelation chapter fourteen is a prediction of Christ in His ultimate triumph. It is also the prediction of the wicked and the pronouncements and visions that support this. Twenty eight times in the Book of Revelation, Jesus is called The Lamb of God.

This 144,000 here is the same ones who were introduced in chapter seven as being sealed. They were sealed by God to be kept safely through the Great Tribulation without losing their lives and still in their earthly bodies. They will go into the millennium without dying. They are tokens of the power of God to keep His people safe.

While this 144,000 are Jews by birth, they are also Christians, saved by the "Blood of the Lamb".

John 14:5 – 6 (5) Thomas said to Him, "Lord, we do not know where you are going, so how can we know the way?" (6) Jesus answered, "I am the Way, the Truth, and the Life. No one comes to the Father except through me."

I believe that **John 14:6** is the most profound statement in the Bible. There is no other way. If you do not believe this statement exactly as it is written, you might as well close this book and read Playboy or some other porn material.

In **John 7:6 – 9** Jesus is praying for His disciples. These are all of the people who believe that Jesus is the Son of God, and accept Him as their Lord and Savior. You may be a great evangelist or someone who works cleaning the church or taking care of the needs of others. But wherever you are at in your Christian walk, other people are watching you, and you should try to reflect the love of Jesus at all times.

In **John 17:6 – 9** (6) I have revealed you to those whom you gave me, out of this world. They were yours and you gave them to me and they have obeyed your word. (7) Now they know that everything that you have given me has come from you. (8) For I gave them the words that you gave me and they have accepted them. They knew with certainty that I came from you, and they believed that you sent me. (9) I pray for them! I am not praying for the world, but for those you have given me, for they are yours.

Contrary to what some limp wristed preachers preach, all people will not be saved. Many will die and go to eternal punishment in Hell. God is a merciful God, but He is also a just and righteous God. You will reap what you sow.

These 144,000 are no different from any other disciples of God. Their main role is to illustrate the power of God to keep them safe during this most awful time of the Great Tribulation.

The sound that was like rushing waters and like a peal of thunder was a demonstration of the divine power of God. The sound also sounds like a harp being played and a new song is being sung. The 144,000 are not singing this song. It is probably being sung by the martyred dead of the Tribulation who are mentioned in **Revelation 7:9 – 10** The song is being sung to the four living creatures and the elders.

The 144,000 are also described as those who have kept themselves pure, clean and redeemed by God. They have been cleaned from all doctrinal and moral impurity, and they follow the Lamb everywhere He goes. Under ordinary circumstances, being married is not regarded as less pure than being single. But during the terrible time of the Great Tribulation, a normal married life will be virtually impossible because of the added responsibility of taking care of a family. In order to serve God without fear of retribution against their families, this 14,000 remain single.

They are found to be holy and blameless. This is an amazing testimony of God protecting His people in the midst of a generation that will be utterly wicked and one that worships Satan. **Revelation 14:6- 13** The Eternal Gospel Proclaimed. (6) Then I saw another angel flying in midair, and he had the "Eternal Gospel" to proclaim to those who live on earth, to every nation, tribe, language and people. (7) He said in a loud voice, "Fear God and give Him glory, because the hour of judgement has come. Worship Him who made the heavens, the earth, the sea and the springs of water." (8) A second angel followed and said, "Fallen! Fallen is Babylon the Great, which made all nations drink the maddening wine of her adulteries." (9) A third angel followed them and said in a loud voice, "If anyone worships the beast, and his image, and receives hi mark on his forehead or on his hand, (10) he too will drink of the wine of God's fury, which has been poured full strength into the cup of His wrath. He will be tormented with burning sulfur in the presence of the Holy Angels and of the lamb. (11) And the smoke of their torment rises forever and ever. There is no rest day or night for those who worship the beast and his image, or for anyone who receives the mark of his name. (12) This calls for patient endurance on the part of the saints who obey God's commandments and remain faithful to Jesus." (13) Then I heard a voice from Heaven say, "Write, Blessed are the dead who die in the Lord from now on." "Yes," says the spirit, "they will rest from their labor, for their deeds will follow them."

The "Eternal Gospel" is the eternal good news of eternal salvation for all people, everywhere, if they will believe in the love, mercy, and the power of God.

God the Redeemer, is also God the Creator, and God the Judge. The wrath of God is shown here as an expression of the mighty power of the sovereign God. God will act with justice and judgement at His right time.

The wrath of God will be with full strength in future judgements, unmixed and undiluted. Until the final judgement, the manifestations of divine wrath have been tempered with redemptive intent. God's wrath in all past judgements has always been with a view of securing repentance. This future wrath will not be mixed with redemptive hope. In its full strength, a fierceness of wrath which has never yet been seen. God's wrath will result in eternal torment for the wicked. It will be too late to cry, "Why me God?" Justice will be served!

The announcement of Babylon's fall does not indicate the end of the Great Tribulation now. It is an announcement of the future destruction of Babylon which is described in Revelation chapter eighteen.

The worshipers of the beast have been previously described as subject to judgement. Though the concept of eternal punishment is difficult for many to comprehend, it is clearly taught in the Word of God. Later revelation in the Book of Revelation indicates that those who die at the time of the second Coming of Christ will go to hades and will not be raised and cast into the lake of fire until after the thousand year reign of Christ on earth.

Those who suffer from the hands of Satan, and wicked men in the Great Tribulation, have their comfort in knowing that their suffering is only temporary. The judgement on those who wickedly persecute them will be forever and ever.

Revelation 14:13 applies only to those who believe, that die in the time of the Great Tribulation. It is not to be a universal recognition of death being a blessing. It reveals that for those who trust in Christ at this time, that death will be better than life. Because they will immediately pass into the blessings of God.

This is the fifth instance of a "voice from Heaven" which gives them a special character. There are two more yet to come and each one is more important and urgent than the previous one. (The number "7" again)

Revelation 14:14 – 20 Judgement at the Second Coming. (14) I looked and there before me was a white cloud, and seated on the white cloud was one "like a son of man", with a crown of gold on His head and a sharp sickle in His hand. (15) Then another angel came out of the temple and called out in a loud voice to him who was sitting on the cloud, "Take your sickle and reap, because the time to reap has come, for the harvest of the earth is ripe." (16) So he who was sitting on the cloud swung his sickle over the earth, and the earth was harvested. (17) Another angel came out of the temple in Heaven, and he too had a sharp sickle. (18) Still another angel who had charge of the fire, came from the alter and called out to him who had the sharp sickle, "Take your sharp sickle and gather the clusters of grapes from the earth's vine, because it's grapes are ripe." (19) The angel swung his sickle over the earth, gathered its grapes and threw them into the winepress of God's wrath. (20) They were trampled in the winepress outside the city, and blood flowed out of the press, rising as high as the horse's gridles for a distance of 1600 stadia.

This picture that John now sees is the Battle of Armageddon, when all the kings of the world gather to do battle against God on "the great day of the Lord". Some believe that these armies will be gathered in the Holy Land to do battle against each other for world supremacy. Whatever reason you want to believe the main thing is all the armies of the world will be gathered there with all of their war equipment. God's battle plan will be revealed in more detail in chapter sixteen.

Revelation 9:13 – 16 states that there will be an army from the east that will cross the Euphrates River. This army will number 200 million mounted troops. The Bible does not state the total number of evil forces that will be gathered to do battle against God on this day.

If we just take the 200 million man army from the east, we can do some simple math. The average adult body contains 11.5 pints of blood. 200,000,000 times 11.5 equals 2,300,000,000 pints of blood. There are eight pints in a liquid gallon. 2,300,000,000 divided by 8 equals 287,500,000 gallons of blood spilled just from the army from the east.

Revelation 16:14 states that this will be a battle on "the great day of God almighty". This will not be a battle that is drawn out over a long period of time. It will be short, swift and devastating. (If you divide 287,500,000 gallons of blood by 24 hours in one day, blood will flow at a rate of 11,979,166 gallons per hour. I believe that this will make it possible for blood to flow as high as a horse's bridle. Remember, this blood is only from the evil forces that came from the east. The evil forces of the whole world will be gathered there, making more blood available.

Manatee Springs is located on the Suwanee River west of Chiefland, Florida. This is one of the largest springs on the Suwanee River and it produces approximately one hundred million gallons of water per day. The springs is located approximately one thousand feet from the river and is fifty to sixty feet wide and three to five feet deep.

There will be almost three times the amount of blood from the army from the east as there is water flowing from Manatee Springs in one day. Add all of the other wicked armies that are gathered there and there will be a sufficient amount of blood to flow a river as deep as a horse's bridle.

Many people do not believe that this will be a literal fulfillment of the scriptures. But, I believe in the God who parted the Red Sea and the Israelites walked through it on dry land. (Exodus 14:13 – 31)

I believe in "The God" that stopped the Jordan River from flowing during its flood stage that allowed the Israelites to cross over into the Promised Land. The scripture does not say that the river just dried up, because it does that during the dry seasons sometimes.

The scripture says that as soon as the feet of the priests, who carried the Ark of the Covenant, touched the water, the water on the upper side began to pile up, while the water on the lower side, flowing to the Sea of Arabah, was completely cut off. **Joshua 3:1 - 17 Joshua** told the people, "Consecrate yourselves, for tomorrow the Lord will do "amazing things" among you."

Do you think that at this time the Israelites may have finally realized how powerful their God really was?

I believe in "The God" who protected the three Hebrew children, Shadrach, Meshack, and Abednego as they walked around in the fiery furnace. The king was so angry because they would not worship him, that he ordered the fire to be seven times hotter than it normally was. It was so hot that it killed the guards on the outside who threw them into the fire. While the king was watching, he saw a fourth person walking around in the fiery furnace with them.

When the king ordered that they be let out of the furnace, there was not one hair scorched on their head, their bodies were not harmed and there was no smell of smoke on them.

If this act could change King Nebuchadnezzar into a believer of "The God" of Shadrach, Meshack, and Abednego, then the power of His love and mercy can change anyone.

Do you think of God coming to rescue only in big time crisis situations? Or, do you think of God getting down in the trenches when one of His people needs a small situation taken care of? How about this power play from God that you probably never heard about?

2 Kings 6:1 – 7 (1) The company of prophets said to Elisha, "Look, the place where we meet with you is too small for us. (2) Let us go down to the Jordan, where each of us can get a pole, and let us build a place there for us to live." And he said, "Go." (3) Then one of them said, "Won't you please come with your servants?" "I will," Elisha replied. And he went with them. (4) They went to the Jordan and began to cut down trees. (5) As one of them was cutting down trees, the iron ax head fell into the water. "Oh my Lord," he cried out, "it was borrowed." (6) The man of God asked, "Where did it fall?" When he showed him the place, Elisha cut a stick and threw it there and made the iron ax head float. (7) "Lift it out," he said. Then the man reached out his hand and took it.

Did the stick cause the iron ax head to float, or was it "God Power"? Is this the God that you know and believe in on a personal level, or do you think that God is too big and too busy to hear your small request?

The "vine" is used to portray both Israel and the church in the Bible. Though the vine was intended to bear righteous fruit, it brought wickedness and evil,, and this calls for the judgement of God.

This chapter deals with primarily the time after the present age of mercy and grace. We, who live in this time, still have the opportunity to believe in God and serve Him, and to receive His mercy and grace. Those who believe in God and serve Him will be "Raptured" before these tragic end time events will overtake the earth.

The nation of Israel covers approximately 8600 square miles. It is about 14 miles wide at its narrow point and about 60 miles wide at its wide point and about 200 miles long. Sixteen hundred stadia is approximately 160 miles. This indicates that the Battle of Armageddon will cover most of the Holy Land.

I do not understand fully how God will accomplish this feat, but I do understand that God will accomplish whatever He desires to accomplish. God has the power and the ability to accomplish whatever He chooses to do.

Revelation 15:1 – 8 Seven Angels with Seven Plagues. (1) I saw in Heaven another great and marvelous sign: Seven angels with seven last plagues, last, because with them, God's wrath is completed. (2) And, I saw what looked like a sea of glass mixed with fire, and standing by the sea, those who had been victorious over the beast and his image and over the number of his name. They held harps given to them by God, (3) and sang the song of Moses, the servant of God, and the song of the Lamb: "Great and marvelous are your deeds Lord God Almighty. Just and true are your ways, King of the ages. (4) Who will not fear you, O Lord and bring glory to your name? For you alone are holy, all nations will come and worship before you, for your righteous acts have been revealed." (5) After this, I looked and in Heaven, the temple that is the tabernacle of the testimony was opened. (6) Out of the temple came the seven angels with the seven plagues. They were dressed in clean shining linen and wore golden sashes around their chests. (7) Then one of the four living creatures gave to the seven angels seven bowls filled with the wrath of God, who lives forever and ever. (8) And the temple was filled with smoke from the glory of God and from His power, and no one could enter the temple until the seven plagues of the seven angels were completed.

God is a just God. His righteousness is ever true, it will never fail. He will not let the righteous fail. He will not let evil win. God's people living in faith, and obedience conquer evil through the power of Jesus Christ. The war has been won!

This third sign is in sequence to the first two signs in **Revelation 12a** In **Revelation 12:1** the sign of the woman represents the nation of Israel. In **Revelation 12:3** the sign of the enormous red dragon with seven heads and ten horns, and seven crowns on his heads, represents the world empire which is controlled by Satan. The sign of the seven angels, the last seven plagues is last because with it, God's wrath is completed.

The number "7" gives the impression of completion or fulfillment of God's judgement on the wicked. These last judgements are more intense and more final than any that precedes them. They are all expression of God's wrath. God's reaction to sin is anger first, then, His wrath comes in the form of His judgements on the wicked.

We see people doing evil things and we ask ourselves the question, "How can God let them get away with doing that?" I can assure you God's chief accountant, Jesus Christ, is keeping a tally, and there will be a "Day of Judgement". It may not be in this lifetime, but justice will be served.

The sea of glass here is probably the same as seen in **Revelation 4:6** and represents The Word of God. It is mixed with fire which is the cleansing power of God to burn away all of our sins, and to purify us for His kingdom. This is the same method used to purify precious metals and make them more valuable.

Those standing beside the sea are described as victorious over the beast and his image. These are the ones who will be saved during The Great Tribulation by leaving Satan and turning to God through His Son Jesus.

Many churches do not preach the "Whole Bible". How many times did God send the Israelites into captivity and destroy their temples? God may forgive us of our sins and short comings, but when we do not act according to His will, He will do whatever He deems necessary to get our attention. Some churches preach that God is only a God of love. There will be a judgement day, and there will be justice for all. To preach anything less than love, judgement and justice, is blasphemy against the "True God". Verses 3 and 4 say that God is a God of justice, truth, holiness and righteousness. We should not fear God, but we should fear His wrath when we do not act according to His ways that He has set for us.

The temple here represents the worship place of the early Israelite nation, where only the high priest could enter the temple and present the sacrifices of the people to God. Jesus was the "unblemished sacrificial Lamb" for all the ages and now we have a one on one relationship with God. I do not need a preacher, priest, or rabbi or anyone else to take my petitions to God. I have an open line anytime I want to dial Him up. He is never too busy to talk to me. I may not always get the answer I want, but He will answer in His time and His wisdom. I am not saying that we should not ask other people to pray for us or for a certain situation. The more prayers that God's people send up, the more God is concerned about us. It does not have to be a long drawn out prayer to impress others. God already knows your need and He knows your heart.

The angels are able to come out of the temple, which is the holy place, because they have no sin. What John is seeing is about to happen. The angels were given the bowls of wrath of God which is about to be poured out on the wicked world. The whole scene is one that is ominous and indicates impending judgements on the world.

The smoke that fills the temple is similar to the cloud that filled the Tabernacle, the Tent of Meeting, just as how God had commanded Moses to set it up. **Exodus 40:34 – 35** (34) Then the cloud covered the Tent of Meeting, and the glory of the Lord filled the Tabernacle. (35) Moses could not enter the Tent of Meeting because the cloud had settled on it and the glory of the Lord filled the Tabernacle.

After the Tabernacle had been duly consecrated to the Lord, His glory filled it in the form of a cloud both day and night. God gave a visible perception of Himself to the Israelites throughout their journeys. When Jesus ascended to Heaven to be with God, He sent the Holy Spirit to live within us and give us a knowing assurance that He will always be with us.

God is glorified when we, His people perceive His greatness and His presence. Do not travel without God as your guiding light. When you travel in the dark, you will stumble and fall.

This place was so holy that even Moses, the man of God who led the Israelites out of bondage in Egypt, could not enter. This expresses how holy these places were then, and how holy they will be again.

Revelation 16:1 Seven Bowls of Judgement. Then, I heard a loud voice from the temple saying to the seven angels, "Go, pour out the seven bowls of God's wrath on the world."

All hell is about to break loose on the whole earth. This chapter sets in motion the wrath of God in dramatic fashion. The sovereign power of God is shown punishing the evil forces of the world. God is in complete control. Evil and wickedness is a harsh reality in this world. One day God will surprise all the forces of evil and destroy them.

High octane adjectives are used throughout this chapter to describe the greatness of what is taking place. Everything about this chapter speaks of the climax as the greatest and most awful period in human history.

There are some similarities between the judgements of the trumpets and the judgements of the seals compared to the judgements of the bowls of wrath. (1) The first one deals with the earth. (2) The next one deals with the rivers (3) and springs of water. (4) The next one deals with the sun. (5) The next one deals with darkness. (6) The next one deals with the Euphrates River. (7) The seventh will be the "grand finale". It will be a comprehensive judgement which includes all that is in the judgement of the trumpets and all that is in the bowls of the wrath of God. The seventh judgement of the bowl of wrath will be capped off by the most severe earthquake the world has ever known and a great hailstorm.

Though the judgements are similar, there are huge differences. The trumpet judgements extend to only one third of the earth, while the bowl judgements affect the whole earth. The scripture reveals that as time progresses, these judgements become more severe and occur in rapid chronological order. The seven bowls of wrath occur in rapid sequence and introduces the situation of the second coming of Christ.

This will be like watching a great fireworks display on July fourth. All of these previous judgements will be great individual occurrences which give you time to say, "wow". These seven judgements will be like the "grand finale" where you just sit in stunned silence watching the awesome power and spectacular fireworks against the night sky. Only, this will be "God Power" on display, not man power. This will happen! Bible prophecy has been fulfilled to its fullest throughout the Bible and will continue to be fulfilled until God says enough.

Revelation 16:2 – 21 The Bowls of Wrath Poured out on a wicked world.

Revelation 16: 2 The First Bowl. The first angel went and poured out his bowl on the land, and ugly and painful sores broke out on the people who had the mark of the beast and who worshiped his image.

The only people who will escape this judgement are those who refuse to worship the beast. This plague will be similar to the plague of boils that Moses put on the Egyptians in **Exodus 9:8 – 12** (8)Then the Lord said to Moses and Aaron, "Take handfuls of soot from a furnace and have Moses toss it into the air in the presence of Pharaoh. (9) It will become fine dust over the whole land of Egypt, and festering boils will break out on men and animals throughout the land." (10) So they took soot from a furnace and stood before Pharaoh. Moses tossed the soot in the air and festering boils broke out on men and animals. (11) The magicians could not stand before Moses because of the boils that were on them and on all the Egyptians. (12) But the Lord hardened Pharaoh's heart and he would not listen to Moses and Aaron, just as the Lord had said to Moses.

There are not many people in the more civilized parts of the world today who have these kinds of boils because of the preventive medicines and better health care in general. But, I remember many people when I was a youngster growing up that would have these boils and many times they would have to go to the doctor to have them lanced. I had several during my early childhood and I remember them being quite painful.

Verse twelve is a preview of the mindset and the attitude of the people during these judgements that God will bring upon the earth during the three and a half years of the Great Tribulation. Even though the people will be suffering greatly, they will still deny and curse God, just as Pharaoh and the Egyptians did. Do you ever think that people are the dumb animals? "Really"

Revelation 16:3 The Second Bowl. The second angel poured out his bowl on the sea and it turned into blood like that of a dead man, and every living thing in the sea died.

This judgement will be similar to the plague of blood in **Exodus 7:14 – 21** when God turned the Nile River into blood making it impossible to drink and killing all the fish. Many believe that this is only and allegorical situation, they believe that it is impossible to turn the sea into blood. How can anyone say that they believe that God created the heavens and the earth and all that is in them and not believe that He could do anything this small?

Exodus 7:14 – 21 The Plague of Blood. (14) Then the Lord said to Moses, "Pharaoh's heart is unyielding, he refuses to let my people go. (15) Go to Pharaoh in the morning as he goes out to the water.

Wait on the bank of the Nile to meet him and take in your hand the staff that was changed into a snake. (16) Then say to him, "The Lord, the God of the Hebrews has sent me to say to you, let my people go, so that they may worship me in the desert. But until now, you have not listened. (17) This is what the Lord says: By this you will know that I am Lord! With the staff that is in my hand, I will strike the Nile, and it will be changed into blood. (18) The fish in the Nile will die and the river will stink; the Egyptians will not be able to drink its waters." (19) The Lord said to Moses, "Tell Aaron, take out your staff and stretch out your hand over the waters of Egypt, over the streams and canals, over the ponds and all of the reservoirs and they will be turned to blood. Blood will be everywhere in Egypt, even in the wooden buckets and stone jars. (20) Moses and Aaron did just as the Lord had commanded. He raised his staff in the presence of Pharaoh and his officials and struck the water of the Nile, and all the water was changed into blood. (21) The fish in the Nile died and the river smelled so bad that the Egyptians could not drink its waters. Blood was everywhere in Egypt.

Since the main principle of this judgement is already recorded history in the Bible, why not believe that God can and will do it again? If He wants to make a bigger pond of blood, He just makes a bigger pond.

Revelation 16:4 – 7 The Third Bowl. (4) The third angel poured out his bowl on the rivers and springs of water and they became blood. (5) Then I heard the angel in charge of the water say: "You are just in these judgements, you who are and were, the Holy One, because you have so judged; (6) for they have shed the blood of your saints and prophets, and you have given them blood to drink, as they deserve." (7) And I heard the alter respond: "Yes, Lord God Almighty, true and just are your judgements."

Attention is called in this judgement to the shedding of the blood of the saints and prophets during the Great Tribulation. The judgements are declared to be true and just. God will have His revenge on this evil world.

Isaiah 34:8 For the Lord has a day of vengeance, a year of retribution, to uphold Zion's cause.

Zion here is the nation of Israel. Sometimes Jerusalem is referred to as the city of Zion. But in this verse, it refers to the whole nation of Israel.

Jeremiah 50:4 – 5 [4] In those days, at that time declares the Lord, the people of Israel and the people of Judah together will go in tears to seek the Lord their God. [5] They will ask the way to Zion and turn their faces toward it. They will come and bind themselves to the Lord in an everlasting covenant that will not be forgotten.

In the days that Jeremiah wrote these words, the Israelites were in bondage to the Babylonians. Jeremiah is prophesying that the Israelites will again turn to God and repent of their sinful ways and call on the Lord to rescue them once again.

John the Revelator is seeing the same thing beginning to happen in this third bowl judgement. There will be people turning to God and asking for forgiveness during the days of the Great Tribulation.

Revelation 16:8 – 9 The Fourth Bowl. [8] The fourth angel poured out his bowl on the sun, and the sun was given power to scorch people with fire. [9] They were seared by the intense heat and they cursed the name of God, who had control over these plagues, but they refused to repent and glorify Him.

We can see here the similarities and differences between the fourth bowl judgement and the fourth trumpet judgement. The fourth trumpet affected the sun, moon and stars, one third of the world was darkened. This will allow the earth to lose much of its light and heat that comes from the sun. The fourth bowl affects only the sun and causes a dramatic increase in heat from it. I believe that this will be like being stranded in the deserts of the world without proper clothing or protection. The word “intense” is one of those action packed adjectives that are frequently used in this chapter to describe the severity of these judgements.

The last phase is a look at how evil and wicked the world will be at this time. The people would rather suffer great despair than to repent of their sins and give God the glory that He deserves.

There are many sins listed in the Bible for which all will be judged. The one sin that I cannot find in the Bible is abortion. You may say that if it is not in the Bible, then it must not be a sin. But, I say that even the pagan nonbelievers were not evil enough to kill their own unborn children.

Is it a fetus or an unborn child? A fetus is something that pregnant women abort from their bodies and throw in the garbage. An unborn baby is "something" that is born to the pregnant woman and grows up to be a real person. When even "so called Christians" say that a woman has the right to do whatever she wants to her body, do they consider that the "thing" inside her womb is a living body? Remember this, things that have no life do not grow! Try planting a dead stick and see how much fruit you pick.

You may ask, "If the world is this evil now, how can it get any worse?" You do not want to be left here when all the Christians are "Raptured". It will be like the law of the jungle, only the strongest will survive.

Revelation 16:10 – 11 The Fifth Bowl. (10) The fifth angel poured out his bowl on the throne of the beast, and his kingdom was plunged into darkness. Men gnawed their tongues in agony, (11) and cursed the God of Heaven because of their pains and sores, but they refused to repent of what they had done. This bowl is a follow up of the first bowl, where the people who had the mark of the beast and worshiped his image were afflicted with painful boils. Now, this bowl affects the throne of the beast and all of his kingdom.

Can you imagine being in so much pain that you would be actually gnawing on your tongue as bad as it hurts when you bite it just one time? The familiar theme of failure to repent is repeated here again. When wicked men are confronted with the power of God, they do not easily come to the place of repentance, but instead they rebel even more against God. They have created this manifestation about themselves, that they are all powerful, and that only they control their destiny and their wants.

Revelation 16:12 The Sixth Bowl. The sixth angel poured out his bowl on the great river Euphrates, and its waters was dried up to prepare the way for the kings of the East. This bowl introduces a number of interesting facts. When the sixth bowl is poured out, the time of the Second Coming of Christ is very near. One of the major features of this period of time is a war in which parts of the world will rebel against the world ruler to try to overthrow his government. The sixth bowl makes its own contribution to this military conflict by drying up the Euphrates River in preparing the way for the kings from the East and their armies to cross.

This will be accomplished by one of two ways: (1) God will supernaturally dry it up by an earthquake or some other means, or (2) they will use the locks and dams that the Russians have already helped build on it. Either way, it will be dried up making it easier for the armies to cross. Because of the rough terrain on the river's edges, it would make it very hard for a large army and its artillery to cross if it was not dried up.

This is the same large military force that John wrote about in **Revelation 9:16**, when he heard that their number was two hundred million. As previously stated, this army will have to come from China, because this is the only country with this much manpower in its military and the only one with enough financial resources to an army this large.

Revelation 16:13 – 14 Demonic Gathering of World Armies. [13] Then I saw three evil spirits that looked like frogs; they came out of the mouth of the dragon, out of the mouth of the beast, and out of the mouth of the false prophet. [14] They are spirits of demons performing miraculous signs, and they go out to battle the kings of the whole world, to gather them for the battle on the "Great Day of God Almighty". These evil spirits that look like frogs, will actually be fallen angels who obey Satan, the world ruler and the false prophets. They are sent out to the whole world to bring together all of the armies of the evil forces of the world to fight this battle in the Holy Land. They will go into this battle believing that whoever comes out, the conqueror will have supremacy over the entire world. They will be correct in their thinking, but little do they know that they will have an unknown adversary. They will ultimately be doing battle against, "The King of Kings and Lord of Lords".

As long as the one world government was in total control, there was no war. The fact that there is now war going on indicates that there will be rebellion against the world ruler toward the end of the Great Tribulation.

Revelation 16:15 "Behold, I come like a thief! Blessed is he who stays awake and keeps his clothes with him, so that he may not go naked and be shamefully exposed."

Many historic disasters have occurred previous to this period of time, and all of them were used to point the world towards God's redemption of His amazing grace and His mercy. As far as God's righteousness is concerned the people will be "naked and shamefully exposed". Justice will be the prevailing factor here, not mercy and grace.

Christ, Himself, proclaims this warning to be prepared just before His second coming. **Luke 12:37 – 40** "Watchfulness" (37) "It will be good for those servants whose master finds them watching when He comes. I tell you the truth, He will dress Himself to serve, will have them recline at the table, and will come wait on them. (38) It will be good for those servants whose master finds them ready, even if he comes in the second or third watch of the night. (39) But understand this: If the owner of the house had known at what hour the thief was coming, he would not have let his house be broken into. (40) You also must be ready, because The Son of Man will come at an hour when you do not expect Him."

If you really study the Bible, you will find that it is a witness unto itself. Each passage of Scripture is backed up by other Scripture. If you read the Bible, you will get out of it the same thing you put into it. "Little"

Revelation 16:16 Then they gathered the kings together to the place that in Hebrew is called "Armageddon". This valley is only fourteen miles wide and twenty miles long. It cannot possibly hold all the millions of troops that will be engaged in this war. So, this will probably be headquarters from which all of the armies will be controlled. The armies will actually be all up and down the Holy Land, which is about two hundred miles in length.

These four verses seem a little contradictory to Revelation thirteen, when Satan, the world leader and the false prophet were compared to the trilogy of the Father, the Son and the Holy Spirit. They were in total control of the world at this time and there were no wars.

The symbolism of staying awake and being dressed means to be prepared at all times. We never know when Satan may try to attack us. Garments are often used in the Bible to refer to righteousness in life. If we keep the garment of the righteousness of God on, Satan cannot penetrate us.

Revelation 16:17 – 18 The Seventh Bowl. "Divine wrath and the Great Earthquake." (17) The seventh angel poured out his bowl into the air, and out of the temple came a loud voice from the throne saying, "It is done!" (18) Then there comes flashes of lightening, rumblings and peals of thunder, and a severe earthquake. No earthquake like it has ever occurred since man has been on earth, so tremendous was the quake.

With this announcement of the seventh bowl, the final judgements on the earth preceding the Second Coming of Christ are revealed. Earthquakes have plagued the world throughout history by destroying much of what man has been able to build. This final earthquake will be more devastating than any in the history of the world.

Revelation 16:19 Destruction of the Great City. The great city split into three parts and the cities of the nations collapsed. God remembered Babylon the Great and gave her the cup filled with the wine of the fury of His wrath. Redemption time is over! Kick butt time has arrived! The loving and merciful God has just put on His robe of judgement and justice.

Isaiah 13:19 Babylon, the jewel of kingdoms, the pride and glory of the Babylonians, will be overthrown by God like Sodom and Gomorrah. This is probably the most profound statement in the Bible that states that God is going to destroy Babylon. Babylon may be a pile of rubbish right now, but it will be rebuilt by the antichrist so God can fulfill this Scripture. If this Scripture is a lie, then the whole Bible is a lie. It is all true or none is true.

Babylon will be rebuilt by the one world government and will become the Capitol of its government. Revelation eighteen confirms that Babylon will be rebuilt then destroyed by God. This prophecy will be fulfilled literally, as will all the other prophecies of the Bible.

Revelation 16:20 -21 Destruction of Islands, Mountains and the Plague of Hail. (20) Every island fled away and the mountains could not be found. (21) From the sky, huge hailstones of about one hundred pounds each fell on men. And, they cursed God on account of the plague of hail, because the plague was so terrible.

The topographical nature of the world will change dramatically as a result of the pending earthquake. The islands will be washed away by huge tidal waves and the mountains will be leveled. Whatever is left after the earthquake will be beaten to a pulp by these huge blocks of ice falling from the sky. As in the previous judgements on the earth by God, mankind still does not repent or confess their sins. Instead, they curse God even more because they recognize that these judgements come from Him. This shows how evil the world really is, they would rather be squashed by huge blocks of ice falling on them than get down on their knees and asking God to forgive them of their sins. Are we getting close to these judgements?

Proponents of global warming theories should read and understand this chapter. Man does not possess the ability to destroy the earth. Destruction of the earth is reserved for God, by God. We should do whatever we can to keep the earth beautiful, because God made us stewards of it. But as smart as we think we are, we cannot prevent wildfires caused by lightening, floods, tornados, hurricanes, hailstorms, droughts, heat waves, or freezes. These things are from God and He has complete control over them. This world will be around until God's final judgement upon it.

All Christians should be thankful that we will be "Raptured", and in Heaven with God when these judgements take place. We will not have to suffer through this period of Great Tribulation. "Thank you God."

Revelation 17:1 – 18 The Woman on the Beast. The Destruction of Ecclesiastical Babylon. The Book of Revelation was written in the order that it was revealed to John. But the events are not always described in chronological order. This is probably most true of Revelation seventeen, which probably occurred during the first three and a half years of the Tribulation.

The best way to establish a difference between chapter seventeen and chapter eighteen is to regard chapter seventeen as the destruction of the Babylonian religions. Chapter eighteen is the destruction of the City of Babylon which will be the capitol of the one world government.

John was invited to witness the punishment of the ecclesiastical Babylon. Using the term "ecclesiastical" does not mean that Babylon represents any kind of "true church", but it is a representative of religious rites and ceremonies. Many of these rites and ceremonies were carried over in part into Roman Catholicism and formed the background for some of their ceremonies. The Babylonian influence is always contrary to the truth and her final hour is described in this chapter. This seventeenth chapter is sort of like a P.S. at the end of a letter to a friend. It may not be in chronological order, but it contains important information which makes the whole big picture more clear.

Revelation 17:1 – 6a (1) One of the seven angels who had the seven bowls came and said to me, "Come, I will show you the punishment of the great prostitute, who sits on many waters. (2) With her the kings of the earth committed adultery and the inhabitants of the earth were intoxicated with the wine of her adulteries." (3) Then the angel carried me away in the desert. There I saw a woman sitting on a scarlet beast that was covered with blasphemous names and had seven heads and ten horns. (4) The woman was dressed in purple and scarlet, and was glittering with gold, precious stones and pearls. She held a golden cut in her hand, filled with abominable things and the filth of her adulteries. (5) This title was written on her forehead: Mystery Babylon the Great. The Mother of Prostitutes and the Abominations of the Earth. (6a) I saw that the woman was drunk with the blood of the Saints, the blood of those who bore testimony of Jesus.

These verses are a picture of what the so called "church" will be like in the end time. When the Rapture occurs, all true believers will be caught up to be with the Lord. But there will be many left who make some profession of faith in Christ, and they will claim to be Christians, but they will not be born again believers. They may talk the talk, but they will not walk the walk. These are the people who will dominate the earth politically and religiously until the last three a half years of the Great Tribulation begins.

After the first three and a half years of the Tribulation, the world leader will break all covenants and proclaim himself to be God. He will no longer need the apostate church to spread his filth and evil ways.

Before we go any farther in our study, there are five words that we must understand and know the similarities and differences between the English and the Bible language. These words are apostasy, prostitute, adultery, abomination, and fornication.

(1) Apostasy

a) The state of having rejected your religious beliefs or your political party or a cause (often in favor of opposing beliefs or causes)

b) Falling away from the Gospel of Jesus Christ

c) It is a revolt against the truth of God's word by a believer

d) It can also describe a group or a church organization that has "fallen away" from the truths of Christianity as revealed in the Bible

The apostate church of the Tribulation period will be guilty of all four of these definitions.

(2) Prostitute:

a) A man or a woman who engages in sexual intercourse for money

b) To offer (a person, especially oneself, or a person's talents) for unworthy causes

Many politicians are guilty of this type of prostitution. They call it horse trading or bartering. But, if you sell your vote for some other persons vote on an unworthy bill that is unable to pass on its own merit for their vote on your unworthy bill, are you not guilty of prostitution? This is what the apostate church will be doing for the one world government. They will dabble just enough religious tidbits to influence some of the people to follow the beast, the false prophet and Satan. It does not have to be sexual favors to be prostitution.

(3) Adultery:

a) Voluntary sexual intercourse between a married man or woman and a partner other than the legal spouse

b) Idolatry, covetousness, and apostasy are often spoken of throughout the Bible as adultery

Seventh Commandment: Thou shall not commit adultery.

First Commandment: Thou shall have no other god before me.

You commit adultery with God when you choose any way or anything other than His way.

(4) Abomination:

a) Anything abominable, greatly disliked, or abhorred

b) A vile, shameful or detestable action, condition or habit

c) Intense loathing – too lazy to work to support yourself or your family

Abomination is used throughout the Bible symbolically to portray sin in general. i.e. Idol worship and ceremonies of the apostate church.

(5) Fornication:

a) The English Dictionary – voluntary sexual intercourse outside of the marriage

b) Law – voluntary sexual intercourse between persons of the opposite sex where one or both are unmarried

c) Bible – sexual immorality in general especially adultery

This word is used more frequently symbolically than in its ordinary sense. It frequently means forsaking God or following after idols.

Prostitute, adultery, and abominations in this passage refer more to spiritual unfaithfulness than to physical unfaithfulness between sexual partners. The church is devoid of any redeeming influence now. It is completely united with the one world government and is working hand in hand with the political powers. The Holy Spirit is gone. There is no one or anything to guide the people to God. God has abandoned the earth for this time period.

The beast is the political empire described in **Revelation 13:1 – 10.** Many believe that the ten horns and seven heads represent a group of people who will promote this one figure as the world leader. The fact that the woman is sitting on the beast indicates that she is working with the beast to obtain their common goals. Their goal is for the entire world to be subjected to their authority.

The "apostate church" represented by the "woman" here is completely supported by the world political power. The woman is wearing the garments of ceremonial religions, in which purple and scarlet were prominent and those garments were decorated with precious stones. These clothes probably represented power because the poor people could not afford clothes like these.

The title written on her forehead links her to the "mystery of Babylon the Great". Remember, at the beginning of this book, I a mystery as: "something when the answer is known, human intelligence cannot fully grasp its meaning".

The influence of Babylon for the evil of the world is supported by scripture from Genesis chapter eleven through the destruction of the rebuilt city of Babylon in Revelation chapter eighteen.

Babylon is the title that covers all "false religions" that claim to be Christian in their content. Many of the "religious "rites and ritual here will be similar to the Old Testament Babylonian churches.

The story of the Tower of Babel is very interesting in how the Babylonian influence or false religions began in the world.

Genesis 11:1 – 9 The Tower of Babel. (1) Now the whole world had one language and a common speech. (2) As men moved eastward, they found a plain in Shinar and settled there. (3) They said to each other, "Come, let's make bricks and bake them thoroughly." They used bricks instead of stone and they used tar for the mortar. (4) Then they said, "Come, let us build us a city, with a tower that reaches to the heavens, so that we may make a name for ourselves and not be scattered over the face of the whole earth." (5) But the Lord came down to see the city and the tower that the men were building. (6) The Lord said, "If as one person speaks the same language they have begun to do this, then nothing they plan to do will be impossible for them. (7) Come, let's go down and confuse their language so they will not be able to understand each other." (8) So the Lord scattered them from there over all of the earth and they stopped building the city. (9) That is why it is called, "The Tower of Babel", because the Lord confused the language of the whole world. From there, the Lord scattered them over the face of the whole earth.

The Lord could have destroyed the tower, but he didn't. He could have destroyed some of the leaders and stopped the construction of the tower, but he didn't. Instead, in His infinite wisdom, he confused their tongues so they could not communicate. Hence, the Tower of Babel could not be built by the babbling Babylonians.

This story is an indication of how smart and educated the people were at this time. The one world government will have much of the same thought pattern. They will believe that they are able to accomplish whatever their wishes and wants are.

The founder of the Babylonian religion was a woman named Semiramis. She was the wife of King Nimrod and obviously had much power and influence. She supposedly conceived a son miraculously, who was given the name, Tammuz. He was portrayed as a savior who would fulfill the promise of a deliverance given to Eve.

This concept of the woman and the child was incorporated into various religious rites and is the background for the tendency in Roman Catholicism to glorify Mary, the Mother of Jesus.

As Christianity came into contact with the Babylonian religions, it created turmoil and confusion in the church. Throughout time there has been a tendency for the church to be anchored in the world instead of God. Modern liberalism has gone even farther in departing from the scriptures. Everything is centered around man and what man wants and what man thinks his rights are.

In the first three and a half years of the Tribulation, Babylonian religions combined with Roman Catholicism, will become the world religion. It may sound Christian in name, but it will not be Christian in context. Those who do come to believe in Christ during this period will be persecuted by the "church". The "church" described here as "the woman" is said to be "drunk with the blood of the saints". Those who do come to Christ in the end time will have double trouble avoiding persecution and death by the political leaders and the church.

This is the main reason that most of the people who do come to Jesus during this time will not be married. By not being married and having families, they will avoid having to watch their families being persecuted and killed.

John was overwhelmed by this revelation and did not fully understand it and it was explained to him by one of the angels. **Revelation 17:6b – 8** (6b) When I saw her, I was greatly astonished. (7) Then the angel said to me, "Why are you astonished? I will explain to you the mystery of the woman and of the beast she rides, which has the seven heads and the ten horns. (8) The beast which you saw, once was, now is not, and will come up out of the Abyss, and go to his destruction. The inhabitants of the earth, whose names have not been written in the Book of Life, from the creation of the world will be astonished when they see the beast, because he once was, now is not, and yet will come."

One of the convincing arguments for worshiping the beast is that he comes back to life after apparent death. This was recorded in **Revelation 13:3** One of the heads of the beast seemed to have a fatal wound, but the fatal wound had been healed. The whole world was astonished and followed the beast.

The Abyss is the home of Satan and the demon world. The whole false religion found in Babylon, is satanic in its origin and closely related to the demon world.

The purpose of the alliance between the woman and the beast is that both are seeking world domination. When this is achieved, the political power will no longer need the religious power to support it.

There are two viable interpretations of the beast "who was, now is not, yet will come".

(1) Some historians and Bible scholars think that it will be the Roman Empire revived.

(2) Others think that the world ruler will be fatally wounded in an assassination attempt and will be miraculously healed by Satan. The important thing is that the world ruler will seem to possess miraculous power and he will be able to deceive many people because of this.

The unsaved of the world, "not in the Book of Life", will be astonished and will put their trust in the world leader and he will be their god.

The angel continues to interpret what John is now seeing. **Revelation 17:9 – 11** (9) "This calls for a mind with wisdom! The seven heads are seven hills on which the woman sits. (10) They are also seven kings. Five have fallen, one is, the other has not yet come, but when he does, he must remain for a little while. (11) The beast who once was, and now is not, is an eighth king. He belongs to the seven and is going to his destruction."

There are several common interpretations of this passage. The statement, "This calls for a mind with wisdom", indicates to me, that we as mere humans may not be capable of interpreting this passage correctly. We may have to wait until its fulfillment to fully understand it.

The most logical explanation is that it refers to the past empires of the world and their kings or rulers. This would include Egypt, Assyria, Babylon, Medo-Persa, Greece, and ancient Rome. As John viewed this scene, the first five empires were history. The Roman Empire was in charge of most of the world that John knew. It is the sixth empire and is the one he refers to as "the one that is". Many Bible scholars believe that the seventh empire will be a revived Roman Empire. This is what John refers to in verse ten, when he stated, "The other has not yet com."

This future empire will be the ten nation kingdom of **Revelation 13:1 and Daniel 7:7 – 8** (7) "After that, in my vision at night, I looked and there before me was a fourth beast – terrifying and frightening and very powerful. It had large iron teeth, it crushed and devoured its victims, and trampled underfoot whatever was left. It was different from all of the former beasts and it had ten horns. (8) While I was thinking about the horns, there before me was another horn, a little one, which came up among them and three of the first horns were up rooted before it. This horn had eyes like the eyes of a man and a mouth that spoke boastfully."

This will be the world ruler who takes over total control of the world from the rulers of the ten nations represented by the ten horns. This pretty much confirms verse eleven which states, "The beast who once was and now is not is an eighth king."

Revelation 17:12 – 13 (12) The ten horns you saw are ten kings who have not yet received a kingdom, but who for one hour will receive authority as kings along with the beast. (13) They have on purpose and will give their power and authority to the beast.

These ten horns which represent the ten kingdoms of the revived Roman Empire have not yet existed and will not exist until the first three and a half years of the Tribulation is completed. It is further revealed that their rule is simultaneous and that it will be for only a short time. They will throw all of their power and authority behind the beast, and he will become the ruler of the whole world. This will make it much easier for him to take over complete control than if he had to take control by force. This will be the same as ten small companies banding together to become an all-powerful conglomerate, with a chief executive that has total control of the company.

Revelation 17:14 They will make war against the Lamb, but the Lamb will overcome them because He is Lord of Lords and King of Kings, and with Him will be His called and faithful followers.

The woman who represents the church, and the beast, who represents the political entity, are both utterly opposed to God and to the people of this time who put their trust in the Lord. But they will not prevail.

Revelation 17:15 Then the angel said to me, "The waters you saw, where the prostitute sits are peoples, multitudes, nations and languages."

Now the angel interprets the statement in verse one, "The great prostitute who sits on many waters." This indicates that the false religion promoted by the woman and the political power of the beast are worldwide.

Revelation 17:16 – 17 (16) "The beast and the ten horns you saw will hate the prostitute. They will bring her to ruin and leaver her naked; they will eat her flesh and burn her with fire. (17) For God has put it in their hearts to accomplish His purpose by agreeing to give the beast their power to rule, until God's words are fulfilled."

This is a tremendous revelation, and truly is a separation of church and state. Somewhere around the midpoint of the last seven years, the apostate church will be no longer useful to the world rulers. The beast, who is the world ruler and the ten nations represented by the ten horns, will destroy the woman and terminate her power and religion.

The purpose behind this is that she will be no longer needed to assist in deceiving the world. The world ruler, who was miraculously brought back to life from a supposedly fatal wound by Satan, will claim to be God. The final three and a half years of the Great Tribulation the world will worship the world ruler and Satan, who is recognized as the power behind the world ruler.

Revelation 17:18 "The woman you saw is the great city that rules over the Kings of the earth."

The character of Babylon is depicted by the woman as a prostitute, but here the reference is to her being a great city, possibly referring to the Vatican, which in the earlier Roman Empire, had ruled over the world as it was known then. The power of the Roman Catholic Church to some degree was the extension of the influence of ancient Babylon throughout history.

Isaiah 13:1–13 A Prophecy against Babylon. (1) An oracle concerning Babylon that Isaiah, son of Amoz saw: (2) Raise a banner on a bare hilltop, shout to them; beckon to them to enter the gates of the nobles. (3) I have commanded my holy ones; I have summoned my warriors to carry out my wrath, those who rejoice in my triumph. Listen, a noise on the mountains, like that of a great multitude. (4) Listen, an uproar among the kingdoms, like nations massing together. The Lord Almighty is mustering an army for war. (5) They came from faraway lands, from the ends of the heavens, the Lord and the weapons of his wrath, to destroy the whole country. (6) Wail, for the day of the Lord is near; it will come like destruction from the Almighty. (7) Because of this, all hands will go limp, every man's heart will melt. (8) Terror will seize them, pain and anguish will grip them, they will writhe like a woman in labor. They will look aghast at each other, their faces aflame. (9) See, the day of the Lord is coming, a cruel day with wrath and fierce anger, to make the land desolate and destroy the sinners within it. (10) The stars of heaven and their constellations will not show their light. The rising sun will be darkened and the moon will not give its light. (11) I will punish the world for its evil, the wicked for their sins. I will put an end to the arrogance of the haughty, and will humble the pride of the ruthless. (12) I will make man scarcer than pure gold, more rare than the gold of Ophir. (13) Therefore, I will make the heavens tremble, and the earth will shake from its place, at the wrath of the Lord Almighty, in the day of His burning anger.

Isaiah 13:19 Babylon, the jewel of the kingdoms, the glory of the Babylonians pride, will be overthrown by God, like Sodom and Gomorrah.

Though much of this prophecy has been fulfilled, it will not be fully fulfilled until the Day of the Lord, which will be the Second Coming of Christ.

Babylon was captured by the Medes, and the Persians, but they did not destroy the city. The city continued to be a large population center through the time of Christ. There was no sudden destruction of the city, but it gradually diminished as a thriving city and today it is mostly in ruins. For this prophecy to be fulfilled completely, Babylon will have to be rebuilt, and become a world power again.

Even in what we call a total eclipse of the sun and the moon, we have never had them refuse to give off light and heat as verse ten depicts that they will not shine.

These passages of scripture are found throughout the Bible and if you just read them they don't seem to have much relevance. But, if you delve into them deeply and study what they really mean, you will know that this is God's divine plan for this world.

This time period does not have to be a period of total darkness to affect the activities of the whole world. We know that as springtime comes and we have longer daylight hours and warmer temperatures, plant life begins to grow faster and animals in the wild begin to be born. The animals are born in the springtime to protect them from the cold winters and also when there is an abundance of food for them to eat.

Many people that grew up on farms in the past know that the lunar signs are controlled by the moon. Crops that bear their fruit above the ground bear more fruit when they are planted on the growing of the moon. Crops that bear their fruit underground, such as potatoes, bear more fruit when planted on the decrease of the moon.

When farmers and ranchers castrated their young pigs, bull calves and young stud horses, they did so when the signs of the moon were in the legs going down to the feet. This was to control blood loss to prevent the animals from bleeding to death.

All hunters and fishermen know the cycles of the moon determine when animals and fish feed. Most sportsmen's magazines provide the lunar tables for their readers to determine the most active feeding times for the animals or fish in their specific time zones. Even the ocean tides are controlled by the cycles of the moon.

When these cycles are altered, even slightly, it will have a tremendous impact on the activities of the world. This is the main reason that it is so important to fully understand these passages.

Revelation 18:1 – 3 "The Destruction of Political Babylon" This prophecy will be fulfilled in its completeness just prior to the Second Coming of Christ. (1) After this I saw another angel coming down from Heaven. He had great authority, and the earth was illuminated by his splendor. (2) With a mighty voice he shouted; "Fallen! Fallen! Is Babylon the great, she has become a home for demons, and a haunt for every evil spirit, a haunt for every unclean and detestable bird. (3) For all nations have drunk the maddening wine of her adulteries. The kings of the earth committed adultery with her, and the merchants of the earth grew rich from her excessive luxuries. Evil empires which pride themselves in wealth, power, and luxury, last only a short time. God is mightier than all earthly powers combined. Jesus will return as, "King of Kings and Lord of Lords."

The prophecy here of the fall of Babylon states that it will become unpopulated, a center for demon power and the home of wild animals. This prophecy has never been fulfilled in the history of the world. Babylon will probably be destroyed by the great earthquake of **Revelation 16:18 – 19** (18) Then there came flashes of lightening, rumblings, peals of thunder, and a severe earthquake. No earthquake like it has ever occurred since man has been on earth, so tremendous was the quake. (19) The great city split into three parts, and the cities of the nations collapsed. God remembered Babylon the Great, and gave her the cup filled with the fury of His wrath.

I wonder if Babylon, being split into three parts has anything to do with the Holy Trinity, God the Father, Jesus the Son and the Holy Spirit. Maybe, each wanted a part in the destruction of this evil city which persecuted and killed their people.

Revelation 18:4 – 8 (4) Then I heard another voice from heaven say, "Come out of her, my people, so that you will not share in her sins, so that you will not receive any of her plagues, (5) for her sins are piled up to heaven, and God has remembered her crimes. (6) Give back to her as she has given; pay her double for what she has done. Mix her a double portion of her own cup. (7) Give her as much torture and grief as the luxury and glory she gave herself. In her heart she boasts, I sit as a queen; I am not a widow, and I will never mourn. (8)Therefore, in one day her plagues will overtake her; death, mourning and famine. She will be consumed by fire, for mighty is the Lord God who judges her.

As **Revelation 17:14** states: "They will make war against the Lamb." As in all wars God's people win some battles to make the people afraid. But, we have the promise of God, that the Lamb will overcome because He is the "King of Kings and Lord of Lords". How appropriate that Jesus can be as gentle as a lamb and yet have more power than all of the kings of the world combined. Gentle enough to make a blind man see, yet strong enough to bind Satan.

God is saying to the world powers, "You have harassed my people long enough. The first team has arrived, now you will get what you deserve. You have been handing out death and heartbreak long enough. Let's see if you can take a double dip of what you have been dishing out. All of this misery and pain that you like to hand out is going to be returned to you in double portions. When one hundred pound blocks of ice begin to fall on your heads, you will have no place to run, because all of the buildings will be on fire."

This is what you call, "being caught between a rock and a hard place."

Those living in Babylon, who believe in God and trust Him, are urged to flee before the destruction begins. Lot was given this same warning to flee Sodom before God completely destroyed it in **Exodus 19:15 – 20.**

The warning of the plagues probably refers back to the seventh bowl of wrath in **Revelation 16:17 – 21.**

The statement that, "her sins are piled up to heaven", probably refers back to the Tower of Babel in **Genesis 11:5.** This was the beginning of a long history throughout time that God had problems with the Babylonians.

The final judgement against Babylon does not come in a long drawn out battle with them. Babylon will be destroyed in one day.

The exhortation to pay her back double for what she has done comes from one of the laws practiced in the Old Testament. If you stole something from someone, you were judged to have to pay them back double what you stole. God will be just. He will follow the law.

When she boasts that, "she is not a widow", she is thinking of all of the dealings and illicit love affairs that she has had with the rulers of the world. She will now receive her payment in full. She will be destroyed and burned to ashes.

Revelation 18:9 – 10 (9) When the kings of the earth who committed adultery with her and shared her luxury see the smoke of her burning, they will weep and mourn over her. (10) Terrified of her torment, they will stand far off and cry; "Woe! Woe! O great city, O Babylon, city of power! In one hour, your doom has come."

This judgement is going to be swift, sure and deadly. When God says, "I have had my fill of these people", all hell is going to break loose on earth.

Revelation 18:11 – 17 (1) The merchants of the earth will weep and mourn over her, because no one buys their cargos anymore, (12) cargos of gold, silver, precious stones and pearls; fine linen, purple, silk and scarlet cloth; every sort of citron wood and articles made, every kind of ivory, costly wood, bronze, iron and marble; (13) cargos of cinnamon and spice, of incense and olive oil, of fine flour and wheat; cattle and sheep; horses and carriages and bodies and souls of men. (14) They will say, "The fruit you longed for is gone from you. All your riches have vanished, never to be recovered. (15) The merchants who sold these things and gained their wealth from her will stand far off, terrified of her torment. They will weep and mourn, (16) and cry out: "Woe! Woe! O great city dressed in fine linen, purple and scarlet, and glittering with gold, precious stones and pearls. (17) In one hour, such great wealth has been brought to ruin.

Every sea captain and all who travel by ship, the sailors and all who earn their living from the sea, will stand far off.

Revelation 18:18 – 19 (18) When they see the smoke of her burning they will exclaim, "Was there ever a city like this great city?" (19) They will throw dust on their heads and with weeping and mourning cry out! "Woe! Woe! O great city, where are all who had ships on the sea and became rich through her? In one hour she has been brought to ruin."

This is another verification of how swift and complete this judgement will be. All of the merchants on the ships waiting to unload their cargo will witness the complete destruction of this evil city. I wonder what their reaction will be. Do you think that there will be some ships put in reverse, making a mass exodus out of this harbor?

Revelation 18:20 – 24 (20)"Rejoice over her, O Heaven! Rejoice saints and apostles and prophets! God has judged her for the way she treated you." (21) Then a mighty angel picked up a boulder the size of a large millstone and threw it into the sea and said; "With such violence the great city of Babylon will be thrown down, never to be found again. (22)The music of harpists and musicians, flute players, and trumpeters, will never be heard in you again. No workman of any trade will ever be found in you again. The sound of a millstone will never be heard in you again. (23) The light of a lamp will never shine in you again. The voice of a bridegroom and bride will never be heard in you again. Your merchants were the world's great men. By your magic spell all the nations were led astray. (2) In her was found the blood of the prophets and of the saints, and all who have been killed on earth.

This prophecy is very specific that all life and events will come to a complete stop when Babylon is completely destroyed. This should prove beyond a shadow of a doubt that Babylon will be rebuilt and become a powerful city in the world again. But, her time will be short. She will be completely destroyed just prior to the Second Coming of Jesus.

God's people must not be deceived and seek to profit or take pleasure in wicked, world power structures. God is mightier than all worldly powers. Just look at a powerful thunderstorm with all of its electrical power, the raw power of a hurricane or tornado or earthquake. Man has not been able to build a structure that God cannot take down.

Salvation is the ultimate goal of God's people. The last days will reveal the true wealth of Christians and leave many people who know only earthly treasures mourning. All of God's people can rejoice that no power on earth can overpower God. God and His people will win in the end.

The first eighteen chapters of Revelation have dealt with God's judgements on an evil world. Now comes the good part. These last four chapters reveal God's blessed plan for His people.

Revelation 19:1 – 3 Prophecy Concerning the Second Coming of Christ. (1) After this I heard what sounded like the roar of a great multitude in Heaven shouting: "Hallelujah!! Salvation and Glory and Power, belong to our God, (2) for true and just are His judgements, He has condemned the great prostitute who corrupted the earth by her adulteries, He has avenged on her the blood of his servants." (3)and again they shouted: "Hallelujah!! The smoke goes up from her forever and ever."

This will be more exciting than being at a college football championship game. This will be sort of like a preview of the things to come. Think about both bands being on the field at the same time, doing a marvelous rendition of the national anthem. You will be awe struck, but when the real team gets here it will be even better.

Revelation 19:4 – 8 (4) The twenty four elders and the four living creatures fell down and worshipped God, who was seated on the throne. And they cried: "Amen, Hallelujah!!" (5) Then a voice came from the throne saying: "Praise our God, all you His servants, both great and small." (6) Then I heard what sounded like a great multitude, like the roar of rushing waters, and like the loud peals of thunder shouting: "Hallelujah!! For our God Almighty reigns! (7) Let us rejoice, and be glad and give Him glory. For the wedding of the Lamb has come, and His bride has made herself ready." (8) Fine linen, bright and clean, was given her to wear.

There are four "Hallelujahs" found in the New Testament and they are all found in the first six verses of this chapter. The word "Hallelujah" means "Praise the Lord".

This tells us that even though there is one more battle to be fought, the war has been won. God's people have been victorious over sin and evil in this world.

I believe that this multitude is the "Raptured Church", God's people. They ascribe to three major attributes to God:

Salvation: God's deliverance from evil.

Glory: God's moral glory in the judgements on sin.

Power: revealed in His judgements on the prostitute, the beast, Satan, and on the evil world, which they controlled.

The smoke of her torment continues forever, refers to the judgement in hades first, prior to the Great white Throne judgement and then in the lake of fire forever.

Revelation 19:9 – 10 (9) Then the angel said to me, "Write: Blessed are those who are invited to the wedding supper of the Lamb." And he added, "These are the true words of God." (10) At this I fell at his feet to worship him. But he said to me, "Do not do it! I am a fellow servant with you and your brothers who hold to the testimony of Jesus. Worship God!! For the testimony of Jesus is the spirit of prophecy."

Some believe that this wedding will take place in Heaven and others believe that it will take place on earth. It really is not relevant where you believe that it will take place, just believe that it will take place.

I believe that it will take place in Heaven. It just doesn't seem likely that Christ will return to earth to marry His bride, the "Raptured Church" which is already in Heaven.

There is a tremendous change in the relationship of God to His people about to take place. Throughout the history of the Bible, God has always said, "I am your God and you are my people." Now comes the day when God changes the relationship to "husband and bride".

Hosea 2:16 "In the day," declares the Lord, "you will call me, my husband, you will no longer call me, my master."

What a beautiful relationship this is going to be. God has always been the provider and the sanctifier for His people. Now each and every Christian "Saint" is going to have a personal relationship with God, just as a wife and a husband have an eternal bond with each other, that is not shared with other people.

Not all people left on earth at this time will be blessed saints. Christ will go into this wedding like a great general. he will be ready to marry his bride and secure her to Him forever, but He knows that He has one more battle to win. He has to capture the false prophet and the beast and throw them into the lake of fire. Then, He has to capture Satan and bind him for one thousand years. If the wedding is to take place on the earth, it will probably be after these two events take place.

One thing is certain, this revelation affirms that God is in complete control of all things and that His children, as believers, will be saved into eternal life by the power of Jesus Christ. Only God deserves worship! Prophecy has its central purpose in revealing the beauty and the righteousness of Jesus Christ.

During Christ's time on earth there were three major steps to a wedding taking place.

(1) There was a marriage contract entered into by the parents of the bride and the parents of the bridegroom would pay a dowry to the parents of the bride. This was the legal marriage and would require a divorce to break the union. This fits naturally into the concept of a wedding when an individual puts his trust in Jesus Christ as his Lord and Savior. He has been bought by the blood of Christ and now belongs to Him.

(2) The second step usually occurred a year or so later. It featured the bridegroom accompanied by his male friends, going to the house of the bride at midnight with a torch parade through the streets. The bride would know that he was coming and would be ready with her hand maidens to join the procession and go back to the home of the bridegroom. This phase of the marriage may be best illustrated in the "Rapture of the Church" when Christ returns to claim the church as His bride and take her to His father's house.

(3) The third phase of the wedding was the wedding supper, "the celebration" which would actually go on for days. This will not be a one day event as we know weddings to be today. This event could and probably will be stretched out over a period of years. No one knows for sure. "Mystery"

The bride is presented as being ready with fine linen, bright and clean, which represents the righteous act of the saints. The bride, "the church", makes herself ready for the coming of the bridegroom, "The Lamb, Jesus Christ", by witnessing, righteous living, and sacrificing themselves to help others in need. The church must always remain morally pure as it waits for the bridegroom.

The consummation of the church as the bride of Christ will complete individual salvation and will result in total righteousness of the church. This will begin the eternal union of the church with Christ, which is the destiny and the hope of the true church.

This is the reason that I believe that the second phase of the wedding, when the bridegroom comes to take the bride home with Him, will be the "Rapture of the Church". After this, there will be no representation of Christ left on earth. Why would He come at another time to claim His bride?

The early church was very confused about the Book of Revelation. They were not sure whether it was about their time frame around the fall of Jerusalem in AD 70, or whether it was about the end of all time on earth. It has been over two thousand years and the debate still goes on today. One thing is for certain and you can put it in your safety deposit box. Jesus Christ is in complete control of all things. His children, as believers, are saved into life eternal with Him, through the power of His shed blood on "The Old Rugged Cross". There is still room for one. God will never run out of space for one of His people.

"Only God deserves worship", not angels, not preachers, not Rabbis, not Father's as called by some churches, not Popes. None of these people deserve worship, whatever their title may be. They cannot mediate our prayers. We pray to God and He hears our prayers. Our communication lines reach the same destination as theirs. I am not saying that we should not ask other people to pray with us or for us. But, when we pray with a repentant heart, our prayers reach just as high as theirs.

Hosea 2:19 – 20 (19) I will betroth you to me forever! I will betroth you in righteousness and justice, in love and compassion. (20) I will betroth you in faithfulness, and you will acknowledge the Lord.

Whether you believe that Hosea was talking about the Israelites in his time or whether he was talking about Christians today does not really matter. What really matters is that we have the same God and we "Christians" are His people also. And if we acknowledge Jesus Christ as our Lord and Savior, God will betroth us in righteousness and justice and in love and compassion.

Ephesians 5:25 – 27 (25) Husbands, love your wives, just as Christ loved the church, and gave Himself up for her (26) to make her holy, and cleansing her by washing with water through the Word, (27) and to present her to Himself as a radiant church, without stain or wrinkle or any other blemish, but holy and blameless.

There is no stain or discoloration, or wrinkle, no blemishes, in every aspect the bride is holy and blameless. This is the result of the sanctifying work of the Holy Spirit at the time of the Rapture when the church is made like Christ. The church is being cleansed during her time on earth by the washing of water portrayed here, this is the Holy Word of God. In preparation for the marriage, our Savior, Jesus Christ died on the cross for His church, and was the perfect sacrifice for our sins.

John was overwhelmed by the revelation in verse 9, "Blessed are those who are invited to attend the wedding supper of the Lamb." He fell at the feet of the angel to worship him and was rebuked by the angel, who stated that he is not to be worshiped.

This passage distinguishes those who are invited to attend the wedding feast from those who are not. Just as many people who know of the bride and groom today are not invited to the weddings or the reception after the wedding, this will be true at this wedding and the celebration after the wedding. Those who know of Christ and do not really know Christ will not get their invitation to attend. If you want to attend this celebration, you had better get on board and start preparing now. Each day without Jesus Christ is a wasted day.

Revelation 19:11 – 16 The Rider on the White Horse (11) I saw heaven standing open and there before me was a white horse, whose rider is called Faithful and True. With justice he judges and makes war. (12) His eyes are like blazing fire and on his head are many crowns. He has a name written on him that no one knows, but he himself. (13) He is dressed in a robe dipped in blood, and his name is the Word of God. (14) The armies of heaven were following him, riding on white horses and dressed in fine lined, white and clean. (15) Out of his mouth comes a sharp sword with which to strike down the nations. He will rule them with an iron scepter. He treads the winepress of the fury of the wrath of God Almighty. [16] On his robe and on his thigh he has this name written. "King of Kings and Lord of Lords".

This is another reason to believe that the wedding ceremony between Christ and His bride, "the church", will take place in Heaven. This event does not look like a bridegroom coming down from Heaven to earth to have a wedding. This is a king and his army coming to claim what is rightfully his. John states very plainly that he is coming to execute his justice on an evil world.

Christ is seen here as bodily leaving Heaven and coming down to earth. The white horse is symbolic of victory. During the Roman Empire, when Christ was on earth, it was customary for the Roman Generals to parade through the streets with their captives following them on foot after a battle had been won. The fact that Christ comes riding on a white stallion indicates that it is time for His victory and judgement on an evil world.

What John recorded is in sharp contrast to the first coming of Jesus, when He came as a baby born in Bethlehem and was placed in a manger. Now, He comes as the conquering King of Kings and Lord of Lords. His total purpose is to make war on an evil world and to execute His justice on it. The fact that He wears many crowns shows that He is the "Almighty King" and that He has power over all the world.

The name written on Him is not revealed. His robe of white linen is dipped in blood. Repentance and forgiveness is past tense now. Jesus has His battle gear on. His robe being dipped in blood probably represents the blood that He shed on the cross for our sin sacrifice, and for His victory over death.

Being called by the name, "Word of God", means that He, like the word of God, expresses who God is.

His army is also riding white horses, and wearing white linen. They are also represented as being victorious, and the white linen signifies their purity.

He is pictured as having a sharp sword in his mouth. This will enable Him to speak "The Word" and to bring judgement on this evil world. He will also rule with absolute power over all, but His rule will be righteous and just.

The symbolism of the winepress, pressing juice out of grapes is used to signify His judgement on the wicked of the world. This is the second time that the word "winepress" is used in the Book of Revelation. Just as a winepress is used to squeeze all of the juice out of grapes, I believe that the fury of God will cause all of the blood of these massive armies to flow out of their bodies. This will literally fulfill **Revelation 14:20**. They were trampled in the winepress outside the city, and blood flowed out of the press, rising as high as the horses bridles for a distance of 1600 stadia.

The Israelites were looking for a king the first time Jesus came. They got a baby. This time they will get their king. This will be a fulfillment of prophecy throughout the Bible. Other scriptures of the Bible bring out more details concerning the Second Coming of Christ.

Zechariah 14:3 – 4 (3) Then the Lord will go out and fight against those nations, as He fights in the day of battle. (4) On that day, His feet will stand on the Mount of Olives, east of Jerusalem, and the Mount of Olives will be split in two from east to west, forming a great valley, with half of the mountains moving north and half south.

This picture distinguishes the Second Coming of Christ from the Rapture, at which time no such event takes place.

Jesus, Himself, described His Second Coming in **Matthew 24:27 – 31** (27) For as lightening that comes from the east is visible in the west, so will be the coming of the Son of Man. (28) Wherever there is a carcass, there the vultures will gather. (29) Immediately after the distress of those days, the sun will be darkened, and the moon will not give its light; the stars will fall from the sky and the heavenly bodies will be shaken. (30) At that time the sign of the Son of Man will appear in the sky and all the nations of the earth will mourn. They will see the Son of Man coming on the clouds with power and great glory. (31) And He will send His angels with a loud trumpet call and they will gather His elect from the four winds, from one end of the Heavens to the other.

This is one event that will not be missed by anyone on earth at this time. You will not need an instant replay, slow motion camera to watch this event for something you may have missed. It will be as visible as lightening in the sky during an electrical storm at night. It will be as impossible to miss as it would be for vultures not to see a squashed armadillo on the road. All the nations of the world will see Jesus return with power and glory. They will be spellbound and in awe of the power and glory that He will return with. Their good times will turn into a time of mourning when they see Jesus returning to claim what is rightfully His. He will not be a baby in a manger or someone they hung on a cruel cross. He will be the all-powerful, "The Almighty God".

Revelation 19:17 – 21 (17) And I saw an angel standing in the sun,
who cried in a loud voice to all the birds flying in midair, come, gather
together for the great supper of God, (18) so that you may eat the flesh
of kings, generals, and mighty men and horses and their riders and
the flesh of all people, free and slave, and small and great. (19) Then I
saw the beast and the kings of the earth, and their armies gathered
together to make war on the rider on the white horse and His army.
(20) But the beast was captured and with him the false prophet who
had performed the miraculous signs on his behalf. With these signs
he had deluded those who had received the mark of the beast and
who had worshipped his image. The two of them were thrown into
the lake of burning sulfur. (21) The rest of them were killed with the
sword that came out of the mouth of the rider on the white horse, and
all the birds gorged themselves on their flesh.

Christ will ride to victory, punishing His enemies and establishing his rule over all creation. Satan will be defeated!! Jesus will rule over His people and He will judge the dead. Unbelievers will be punished, while believers will live eternally with Jesus in the New Jerusalem. God's church can depend on Jesus. The pure and faithful will receive their rewards from Him.

The fact that the angel speaks with a loud voice as in previous events throughout Revelation signifies that something great is about to happen. The invitation to the birds flying in midair to partake of the feast of the dead bodies of the army that has been killed in this battle is in direct contrast to the invitation given those who are invited to attend the wedding supper of The Lamb.

These terrible judgements that are inflicted on the armies of the world who are gathering to make war against Jesus and His army from Heaven proves that God does not respect worldly authority. From the highest ranking generals to the lowest privates or foot soldiers, there will be no escape from the wrath of God.

The only people who escape death in this battle are the beast and the false prophet. They are captured. This is very significant, because throughout the history of the world, great men of battle had rather be killed on the battlefield than to be captured. If you allow yourself to be captured it seems to some that you lose some of the allure of your mystique and power.

The capture of these two is very significant. God does not have to extract information from them as we try to get information from people that we capture in wars. God's plan for these two is worse than being killed on the battlefield. Remember that the Romans paraded their captives through the streets after they had been captured in battle.

Picture this: Jesus will be riding this magnificent white stallion with a rope tied to the beast and the false prophet, leading them down this long straight path. This will be the first and last time that these two will travel on the straight and narrow way. In the distance they can see the lake of fire and as they get closer, they begin to smell the smoke of the burning sulfur. And, as they get even closer, they begin to feel the intense heat.

When Jesus throws them into the lake of fire, they do not die immediately. **Revelation 20:10** tells us that the beast and the false prophet are still in the fire, and still burning one thousand years later.

Remember in chapter eleven I told you that the communication satellites that we use today will show this scene of the two witnesses that are killed and left in the streets for three and a half days before they are lifted up into Heaven. These same satellites will be recording this procession as these two are being led by Jesus to their ultimate justice. The world will not have to wonder what really happened to these two. They will witness scripture being fulfilled.

I wonder what their thought process will be as they are being led down this long straight path to their ultimate destination.

The story of the rich man and Lazarus is another example that those who are thrown into this fiery lake of burning sulfur will be tormented forever.

Luke 16:19 – 26 (19) There was a rich man who was dressed in purple and fine linen and lived in luxury every day. (20) At his gate laid a beggar named Lazarus, covered with sores (21) and longing to eat what fell from the rich man's table. Even the dogs came and licked his sores. (22) The time came when the beggar died, and the angels carried him to Abraham's side. The rich man also died and was buried. (23) In hell, where he was in torment, he looked up and saw Abraham far away, with Lazarus by his side. (24) So he called to him, "Father Abraham, have pity on me, and send Lazarus to dip the tip of his finger in water and cool my tongue, because I am in agony in this fire." (25) But Abraham replied, "Son, remember that in your lifetime you received good things, while Lazarus received bad things, but now he is comforted and you are in agony. (26) And besides all of this, between us and you, a great chasm has been fixed, so that those who want to go from here to there cannot, nor can anyone cross over from there to us."

These two passages are very similar in their content concerning torment in the lake of fire. God always supplies two witnesses to anything that He does. This is in compliance with the Old Testament laws that it took two witnesses to convict someone in a court of law.

Revelation 20:1 – 3 The Binding of Satan (1) And I saw an angel coming down out of Heaven, having the key to the Abyss and holding in his hand a great chain. (2) He seized the dragon, that ancient serpent who is the devil or Satan, and bound him for one thousand years. (3) He threw him into the Abyss, and locked and sealed it over him, to keep him from deceiving the nations anymore, until after the thousand years were ended. After that he must be set free for a short time.

John saw Satan being bound for one thousand years and he was thrown into the Abyss, which is the home of Satan and the fallen angels. The opening was sealed and locked. This makes Satan powerless to interfere during the millennial reign of Christ.

God cannot be any more clear about the millennial reign of Christ than He is in these three verses. This passage makes clear that Satan is not simply restricted in some way, as some teach, but that he is totally inactive for one thousand years, until he is released from this prison by God. The American Civil Liberties Union lawyers or none of their sleazy cohorts will be able to get him released on charges that the one thousand year prison sentence is cruel and inhumane punishment.

Many believe that this is being fulfilled during our present age now. This theory is completely debunked by **I Peter 5:8** "Be self-controlled and alert. Your enemy, the devil prowls around like a roaring lion looking for someone to devour."

Though Satan is restricted by God in his power now, he is still able to interfere and lead people astray. During the one thousand years in prison he will be completely helpless. God probably will not even unchain him to eat. God has the unique power to sustain him in any way that He chooses. Just think how much more devastating his sentence will be if he has to sit chained up in prison and watch the people that he tormented walking around praising God and eating good food.

Revelation 20:4 – 6 The Resurrection of the Tribulation Saints.(4) I saw thrones on which were seated those who had been given authority to judge. And I saw the souls of those who had been beheaded because of their testimony for Jesus and because of the word of God. They had not worshipped the beast or his image and had not received his mark on their forehead of hands. They came to life and reigned with Christ a thousand years. (5) The rest of the dead did not come to life until after the thousand years were ended. (6) Blessed and holy are those who have part in the first resurrection. The second death has no power over them, but they will be priests of God and Christ and will reign with Him for one thousand years.

This one thousand year reign of Jesus on earth is prophesied six times in the first seven verses of this chapter. I do not understand how God can make it any more clear that this is going to happen. It is referred to by many as the Millennium. There are four different views of the Millennial beliefs taught throughout the Christian church by Bible scholars, theologians, preachers and anyone else who cares to voice their opinion. They are: A millennialism, Post millennialism, Dispensational Pre millennialism and Historic Pre millennialism.

These variations of opinions arise from different views on the interpretations of key Biblical verses. Each view is held by people with strong convictions on how the Bible should be interpreted. This is like having several people write a report on an event that they all saw happen at the same time. They will give varying interpretations according to what they think are the key components of what they saw. This does not make anyone of them right or wrong, this is human nature. God did not make us all to act alike or think alike.

These differences of interpretation probably will not be settled until Christ returns, which they all agree on. This is the key to the whole millennial belief. Christ will return to earth to setup a physical kingdom on earth.

Since I tend to agree to the teaching of dispensational pre millennialism, I will discuss it, and if you are interested in the other three, you can find them in many Bible commentaries or on the internet.

Even among dispensational pre millennialism believers, there are some disagreements. Some believe that Christ intended to establish His kingdom on earth at His first coming, but could not do so because of unbelief, so He instituted the church age of mercy and grace. Most believe that it was God's plan from the beginning that Jesus Christ would be the perfect sacrificial lamb to pay for the sins of all of those who are believers.

All dispensational pre millennialism believers, believe that after the Rapture of the church and the Tribulation period, Christ will return to earth and by force will establish His kingdom on earth. It will take force to kill all of the armies that are gathered to do battle, to throw the false prophet and the beast into the lake of fire, and to chain up Satan for one thousand years. They will not give up their regime without a fight.

The people who are killed during the Great Tribulation period for not worshiping the beast are now resurrected and honored because they did not receive the mark of the beast. The purpose of their resurrection at this time is for them to reign with Christ during the

Millennial. This resurrection is slated as "the first" because it is before the resurrection of the wicked. Jesus was the first person to be resurrected.

This is what Jesus told His disciples in **Luke 22:29 – 30** (29) "And I confer on you a kingdom, just as My Father conferred one on me, (30) so that you may eat, and drink at my table in My Kingdom, and sit on thrones, judging the twelve tribes of Israel."

This is even more proof that the resurrected saints that are with Jesus when He returns to claim His Kingdom, will have some form of body. They will be joined by the people who are killed during the Tribulation period because of their belief in God.

I do not see how anyone can even speculate that we will be in some sort of spirit form. It is pretty hard for me to visualize spirits sitting around a table eating and drinking and judging the people who are brought before them.

Those who reign with Christ will not have equal status, but will be subject to Christ and will be acting on His behalf. It is absolutely clear in the Scriptures, that the Millennial reign of Christ on earth will begin with the Second Coming of Christ, and will end with judgement on the world and the creation of a new heaven and a new earth.

One of the first to prophesy of the Millennial was King David, Son of Jesse.

Psalm 72:1 – 19 (1) Endow the king with your justice, O God, the royal son with your righteousness. (2) He will judge your people with righteousness, your afflicted ones with justice. (3) The mountains will bring prosperity to the people, the hills the fruits of righteousness. (4) He will defend the afflicted among the people, and save the children of the needy, He will crush the oppressor!! (5) He will endure as long as the sun, as long as the moon, through all generations. (6) He will be like rain falling on a mown field, like showers watering the earth. (7) In His days the righteous will flourish, prosperity will abound till the moon is no more. (8) He will rule from sea to sea, and from the river to the ends of the earth. (9) The desert tribes will bow down before Him, and His enemies will lick the earth. (10) The kings of Tarshish, and of distant shores will bring tribute to Him, the kings of Sheba and Seba will present Him with gifts. (11) All kings will bow down to Him, and all nations will serve Him. (12) For He will deliver the needy who cry out, the afflicted who have no one to help. (13) He will take pity on the weak and the needy, and save the needy from death. (14) He will rescue them from oppression and violence, for precious is their blood in His sight. (15) Long may He live! May gold from Sheba be given to Him, may people ever pray for Him, and bless Him all day long. (16) Let grain abound throughout the land, on the tops of hills may it sway. Let its fruits flourish like Lebanon, let it thrive like the grass of the field. (17) May His name endure forever: May it continue as long as the sun; all nations will be blessed through Him, and they will call Him blessed. (18) Praise be to the Lord God, the God of Israel, who alone does marvelous deeds. (19) Praise to His glorious name forever, may the whole earth be filled with His glory. Amen and Amen.

This concludes the prayers of David, Son of Jesse.

This future time, the Millennial, is described by King David as flourishing, the government as righteous and abundant peace is promised as long as the moon endures. All the kings of the earth will bow down before Christ and His rule will be from sea to sea. The earth will be filled with the glory of God. The major factors of the Millennial will be God's absolute power, the perfect and righteous government and perfect circumstances on earth.

Throughout the Old Testament, Israel is prophesied to have a very important role in the Millennial. **Ezekiel 20:33 – 44** (33) As surely as I live declares the sovereign Lord, I will rule over you with a mighty hand and an outstretched arm and with outpoured wrath. (34) I will bring you from the nations, and gather you from the countries where you have been scattered- with a mighty hand, and an outstretched arm and outpoured wrath. (35) I will bring you into the desert of the nations, and there face to face, I will execute judgement upon you. (36) As I judged your fathers in the land of Egypt, so will I judge you declares the sovereign Lord. (37) I will take note of you as you pass under my rod, and I will bring you into the bond of the covenant. (38) I will purge you of those who revolt and rebel against me. Although I will bring them out of the land where they are living, they will not enter the land of Israel. Then you will know that, I am the Lord!! (39) As for you O house of Israel, this is what the sovereign Lord says, "Go and serve your idols, every one of you. But afterward you will surely listen to me and no longer profane my name with your gifts and idols.

(40) For on my holy mountain, the high mountain of Israel, declares the sovereign Lord, there in the land, the entire house of Israel will serve me, and there I will accept them. There I will accept your offerings, and your choice gifts, along with all your holy sacrifices. (41) I will accept you as fragrant incense when I bring you out of the countries where you have been scattered, and I will show myself holy among you, in the sight of the nations. (42) Then, you will know that I am the Lord! When I bring you into the land of Israel, the land that I had sworn to give to your fathers. (43) There you will remember your conduct, and all the actions by which you have defiled yourselves, and you will loathe yourselves for all the evil you have done. (44) You will know that I am the Lord, when I deal with you for my name's sake, and not according to your evil ways, and your corrupt practices, O house of Israel, declares the sovereign Lord."

The Lord uses the first person noun "I" twenty one times in these twelve verses. He says "I will" eleven times. He uses the term "sovereign Lord" four times. He says three times, "you will know that I am the Lord". I believe that God was emphasizing to the Israelites at that time that He was in charge then and in the future.

God selected Israel to have a people who would worship only Him and would know Him in an intimate relationship as their only God. He worked in love and in wrath to lead them to freely conform to His will.

God delivered Israel with a mighty hand and an outstretched arm over the Red Sea when they escaped from Egypt. He finally had to judge Israel as he had judged Egypt.

God's judgement on His people is not a rare occurrence. Throughout the Old Testament He is continually punishing the Israelites for following practices which are contrary to His ways and His values. His judgement is not a total destruction, but a purging of rebels and unbelievers.

God gives us salvation by accepting us as we serve Him. Salvation requires our acceptance of God's acceptance. When God accepts us as His own, we must respond accordingly. Salvation is not a one way street.

When Jesus returns as "king of kings and Lord of Lords" He will be accepted by the nation of Israel as their messiah, whom they have been looking for over two thousand years.

Jerusalem is recognized in the Old Testament as being the Center of Jesus' rule on earth when He returns. **Isaiah 2:2 – 5** (2) In the last days, the mountain of the Lord's temple will be established as chief among the mountains, it will be raised above the hills and all nations will stream to it. (3) Many peoples will come and say, "Come, let us go up to the mountain of the Lord, to the house of God of Jacob. He will teach us His ways so that we may walk in His paths. The law will go out from Zion, the word of the Lord from Jerusalem. (4) He will judge between the nations and will settle disputes for many peoples. They will beat their swords in plowshares, and their spears into pruning hooks. Nation will not take up sword against nation, nor will they train for war anymore. (5) Come, O house of Jacob, let us walk in the light of the Lord."

Isaiah foresaw a day of universal peace among all nations. Christians view this prophecy as only being fulfilled through Jesus Christ the Lord. God was preparing the world for the salvation of humankind through His inspired prophets.

Obeying God means walking in his paths. Walking in His paths includes believing in His son as Lord and Savior and moral behavior and divine teaching will be a major characteristic of the messianic age. It will include justice, righteousness, harmony and universal peace.

Revelation 20:7 – 9 The Final Rebellion Against Christ (7) When the thousand years are over, Satan will be released from his prison, (8) and will go out to deceive the nations, in the four corners of the earth, Gog and Magog to gather them for battle. (9) They marched across the breadth of the earth and surrounded the camp of God's people, the city He loves. But fire came down from Heaven and devoured them.

One of the major questions asked about the teachings of Revelation is why will Satan be released after being bound and held powerless in prison for a thousand years? The answer is: through history, when mankind is left alone to their own desires and devices, they will choose to sin against God. Even though the Millennial will provide a perfect environment for humanity with abundant revelation of God's power, the evil heart of man will reject God and follow Satan when given the opportunity. The immediate rewards of the world always looked better to mankind.

Some have confused this war with the war of **Ezekiel 38 and 39**, but it is more in line with what we now call the Battle of Armageddon. Ezekiel prophesize that armies from all the nations of the world will be gathered to do battle and they will be completely destroyed by God and the birds and the wild animals will eat their flesh. This is more in line with **Revelation 16 through 19**. This passage in verse nine clearly tells us that there will be no bodies to bury or flesh for the birds and the wild animals to eat. The fire that comes down from Heaven not only kills all of these people, but it completely devours them.

Revelation 20:10 Satan Cast into the Lake of Fire. And the devil, who deceived them, was thrown into the lake of burning sulfur, where the false prophet and the beast had been thrown. They will be tormented day and night forever and ever.

Satan was thrown into the lake of burning sulfur for his wickedness and for deceiving God's people. Satan's fate was sealed all the way back in **Genesis 3:15** And I will put an enmity between you and the woman, and between your offspring and hers; He will crush your head and you will strike his heel.

The woman is Mary and her offspring is Jesus. The serpent's offspring is Satan. The striking of His heel is the crucifixion of Jesus on the cross. The crushing of the serpent is the resurrection from the grave of Jesus on the third day. This is followed by the binding of Satan and him being in prison for one thousand years. The philosophy of three strikes and you are out is the throwing of Satan into the lake of fire where he will be tormented forever and ever. Eternal judgement or eternal glory, you have a choice.

Revelation 20:11 – 15 The Great white Throne Judgement (11)Then I saw a great white throne and Him who was seated on it. Earth and sky fled away from His presence and there was no place for them. (12) And I saw the dead, great and small, standing before the throne and the books were opened. Another book was opened which is the Book of Life. The dead were judged according to what they had done as recorded in the books. [13] The sea gave up the dead that were in it, and death and Hades gave up the dead that were in them, and each person was judged according to what he had done. [14] Then, death and Hades were thrown into the lake of fire. The lake of fire is the second death. [15] If anyone's name was not found written in the Book of Life, he was thrown into the lake of fire.

This is the resurrection of the wicked dead of **Revelation 20:5** God's people have already been resurrected in **Revelation 20:4** They came to life and reigned with Christ for a thousand years.

Revelation 20:5 The rest of the dead did not come to life until the thousand years had ended.

The word "throne" appears in Revelation over thirty times. This throne is different from all of the others which were either in Heaven or on earth. This throne is pictured as being in space and is occupied by Jesus Christ Himself.

Revelation 20:11b Earth and sky fled away from His presence and there was no place for them.

Jesus will be the final judge!!

John 5:22 – 23 [22] Moreover, the Father judges no one, but has entrusted all judgement to the Son, that all may honor the Son as they honor the Father. [23] He who does not honor the Son, does not honor the Father who sent Him.

God has revealed that physical death is not the end of life. All of the dead will be judged and will have to give an account of their lives on earth.

Revelation 20:14 Then death and Hades were thrown into the lake of fire. The lake of fire is the second death.

Those who do not belong to God and whose names are not written in the Book of Life will suffer torment forever and ever.

The lake of fire is a synonym for hell. This second death is the final separation from God. All people die once, a physical death. This second death for the unbeliever will be worse than the physical death.

Special mention is made of the sea giving up the dead in it. Bodies lost at sea disintegrate and are scattered from sea shore to sea shore. This is no problem for an all- powerful God who will raise their bodies the same as he raises the bodies of those buried on land.

There is a major difference between Hades and the lake of fire. Hades is the place of the dead and their resurrection. The lake of fire is the final destination of all of those who are unsaved.

Like the righteous, the unsaved are given bodies which will not be destroyed. But, the righteous will receive bodies that are holy and suited for being in the presence of God forever. The unrighteous will receive bodies that are suited for eternal punishment forever. Even though they are thrown into the lake of fire, they will never burn up. They will burn forever!! If the beast and the false prophet are still intact and still burning after one thousand years, these unrighteous will likewise continue to burn forever.

Scriptural revelation limits the destiny of mankind to two places, Heaven or the lake of fire. You get to make the choice. Which will it be?

Revelation 21:1 – 4 The New Heaven and New Earth and New Jerusalem (1) Then I saw a new Heaven and a new earth, for the first Heaven and the first earth had passed away, and there was no longer any sea. (2) I saw the Holy City, the New Jerusalem coming down out of Heaven from God, prepared as a bride, beautifully dressed for her husband. (3) And I heard a loud voice from the throne saying, "Now the dwelling of God is with men and He will live with them. They will be His people and God Himself will be with them and He will be their God. (4) He will wipe every tear from their eyes. There will be no more mourning or crying or pain, for the old order of things has passed away.

All of the global warming theorists should read and comprehend these four verses. No matter how many nuclear weapons we explode or what we pump into the air, mankind will not destroy the earth. God has reserved this for Himself and in His time. This does not mean that we should not do everything that we can to protect the earth and its beauty, because God made us His stewards of it.

God originally made the earth to be the home for His people that He created to have fellowship with Him. But sin entered into mankind and changed it into a place of rebellion and alienation from God. Since Adam and Eve, God has been working to reverse the terrible consequences that sin has brought to humans.

History on this earth will end! That is God's plan! All things will be made new! Out of the Heavens comes a new city: Jerusalem!!

The only physical revelation given of the new earth and new Heaven is that there will no longer be any sea. Today's earth is approximately eighty percent covered by water.

Without any explanation, John states that the New Jerusalem comes down out of Heaven. Many people say this is physically impossible. They are again trying to equate God to mankind. This does not work. There is no comparison. God is not limited in His ability to accomplish His things. This will be no harder for God to accomplish than the parting of the Red Sea or stopping the flow of the flooded Jordan River to allow the Israelites to crossover into the Promised Land.

The "how" it happens does not matter. The "why" it happens is what matters. Because it is God's plan for His people. If you believe in a God that you cannot see, why not believe in a "New Jerusalem" coming down out of the sky.

The New Jerusalem in the new earth is God providing a new and happy home for the believers of all ages. God will live with His people in the New Jerusalem. It will be His temple. We will no longer have to believe or worship in faith. We will be able to spend eternity with God.

When John says, "There will be no more death, mourning or crying or pain", it simply means that we will spend our time praising and worshiping God.

Revelation 21:5 – 8 (5)He who was seated on the throne said, "I am making everything new!!" Then He said, "Write this down, for these words are trustworthy and true." (6) He said to me, "It is done! I am the Alpha and the Omega! The Beginning and the End! To him who is thirsty, I will give drink without cost from the spring of the water of life. (7) He who overcomes will inherit all of this, and I will be his God and he will be my son. (8) But, the cowardly, the unbelieving, the vile, the murderers, the sexually immoral, those who practice magic arts, the idolaters, and all liars, their place will be in the fiery lake of burning sulfur. This is the second death!"

You can believe that when God told John specifically to write something down, He was about to reveal something of great magnitude to him.

The words, "Alpha and Omega" are the first and last letters of the Greek alphabet. God was simply saying, "I was here first, I have always been here, I will always be here, and I will be the last one to leave. Without me there is nothing."

The wonderful gift of salvation by grace and the drinking of water from the spring of life are just part of the wonderful provisions God has made for us Christians who put our trust in Him. God promises that all who overcome by faith will inherit all of His wonderful kingdom, and that He will be their God and they will be His son. The Almighty God has always had and will always have ultimate control over our world. Those who live their lives according to God's righteous plan in verse seven will receive their rewards from a loving God.

Those who live their lives in sin as recorded in verse eight will receive their just judgement. This does not mean that if you have sinned that you cannot be saved. But, you must ask God to forgive you of your sins and repent, which is to turn away from sin. Those who do not repent or respond to faith in Christ will have to face the fact that their destiny is a second death in the fiery lake of burning sulfur.

Born once.........Die twice

Born twice.........Die once

You have a choice!

Revelation 21:9 – 10 The New Jerusalem (9) One of the seven angels who had the seven bowls full of the seven last plagues came and said to me, "Come, I will show you the bride, the wife of the Lamb." (10) And he carried me away in the spirit to a mountain great and high, and showed me the Holy City, Jerusalem, coming down out of Heaven from God.

The bride of Christ is composed of the church of the present age. This is the body of people who have accepted Jesus as their Lord and Savior. The relationship of calling the church, the bride, is to show the beauty of being holy, pure and clean.

John was allowed to witness a new creation, made perfect by God, designed and working as he had planned for mankind from the beginning in the Garden of Eden.

Revelation 21:11 – 21 (11) It shown with the glory of God, and its brilliance was like that of a very precious jewel, like a jasper, clear as crystal. (12) It had a great high wall with twelve gates, and with twelve angels at the gates. On the gates were written the names of the twelve tribes of Israel. (13) There were three gates on the east, three gates on the north, three gates on the south, and three gates on the west. (14) The wall of the city had twelve foundations, and on them were the names of the twelve apostles of The Lamb. (15) The angel who talked to me had a measuring rod of gold to measure the city, its gates and its walls. (16) The city was laid out in a square, as long as it was wide. He measured the city with a rod and found it to be 12,000 stadia in length and as high and wide as it was long. (17) He measured its wall and it was 144 cubits thick, by man's measurement, which the angel was using. (18) The wall was made of jasper, and the city of pure gold, pure as glass. (19) The foundations of the city walls were decorated with every kind of precious stone. The first foundation was jasper, the second sapphire, the third chalcedony, the fourth emerald, (20)the fifth sardonyx, the sixth carnelian, the seventh chrysolite, the eighth beryl, the ninth topaz, the tenth chrysoprase, the eleventh jacinth, and the twelfth amethyst. (21) The twelve gates were twelve pearls, each gate made of a single pearl. The great street of the city was of pure gold, like transparent glass.

The glory of God represents the shining radiance of God which makes all other sources of light seem insignificant to the brilliance of God. The best way to even comprehend the beauty of this city is to watch a sunrise or a sunset in the mountains. You can see the beauty of God as the light grows brighter in the sunrise or as it grows dimmer in the sunset. Only God can provide this beauty.

In the New Jerusalem, God will be fully disclosed to His people in the full radiance of His glory. We will no longer worship a God that we cannot see.

The angel measured the city and its measurements were 12,000 stadia wide and 12,000 stadia long. But, it was also as high as it was long or wide. The land area of this city is about fourteen hundred miles wide and fourteen hundred miles long. This equates to an area of 1,960,000 square miles. This city would cover an area approximately from Tampa to Boston, to Minneapolis, to Brownsville, Texas and back to Tampa, Florida.

Some say that this is not enough room for all the Christians and Old Testament saints to live in. But don't forget this city is also fourteen hundred miles high.

Most of the tallest buildings in the world are less than a quarter mile high. This means that the buildings in the New Jerusalem will be fifty six hundred times taller than the tallest buildings of today's standards.

Most commercial airlines fly at an altitude of about thirty five or thirty six thousand feet. This city will be two hundred times higher than they fly.

There is only one architect and one builder who can accomplish this feat. God Almighty Himself!

The wall is said to be 144 cubits thick and is as high as it is thick. A cubit is the length of a man's arm from his elbow to the tip of his index finger. This is an average of about twenty inches, which would make this wall approximately two hundred and forty feet wide and it will be as high as it is wide.

The number "twelve" is very prominent in the description of the New Jerusalem. There are twelve gates, twelve angels, twelve tribes of Israel, twelve foundations, twelve apostles, twelve pearls and twelve kinds of fruits in **Revelation 22:2.** Throughout the Bible the number "seven" represents completion or perfection. There are seven "twelves" listed here. This simply means that God has completed this city and it is perfect in every way.

The fact that the twelve gates are named for the twelve tribes of Israel indicates that the Israelites will be a major part of the population of this city.

The wall of the city has twelve foundations with the name of one of the twelve apostles on each one of them.

After putting all of the facts together, we can conclude that the New Jerusalem will be the new home of all saints (believers) of all ages, and God Himself will be there.

Hebrews 12:22 – 24 (22) But, you have come to mount Zion, to the heavenly Jerusalem, the city of the living God. You have come to thousands upon thousands of angels in joyful assembly, (23) to the church of the firstborn, whose names are written in Heaven. You have come to God, the judge of all men, to the spirits of righteous men made perfect. (24) To Jesus the mediator of a new covenant, and to the sprinkled blood, that speaks a better word than the blood of Abel.

This passage of scripture brings us to an awesome experience of the New Covenant promises through the life, death, and resurrection of Jesus. Most of the Old Testament Covenant was based on fear of God. Now Jesus is our mediator of the New Covenant. He shed His blood on Calvary to cover our sins. To refuse the Gospel is to face the judge for punishment.

People such as Abel died unjustly. Though their faithfulness sets a good example for us to follow, what they did for us cannot compare to the atoning blood shed by Jesus, which established a New Covenant and paid for all of our sins.

In the New Jerusalem there will be thousands upon thousands of angels, the church, believers of Jesus Christ, and all the saints of the Old Testament. They will be joined in the City by God the Father, God the Son, and God the Holy Spirit.

The foundations of the city walls are each made with a beautiful and precious stone. The fact that they are all different, yet when blended with each other, they are glowing with the glory of God, represents the inclusiveness of God's love for all of His people. We may all be different as individuals, but when we are blended with God, we make up a glorious body. "The Church – The Bride of Christ".

If you want just a taste of what John was seeing, just watch a beautiful sunrise or sunset as they change colors. Or, watch a white puffy cloud in the far distance as God touches it and turns it into a powerful electrical storm with all of its colors and beauty.

I am as colorblind as God ever made a man, but I am in awe of the awesomeness of the portraits that God paints in the sky. If what I see is just a taste of what John saw, I want to be in that number, "When the Roll is Called up Yonder".

Revelation 21:22 – 27 (22) I did not see a temple in the City, because the Lord God Almighty and the Lamb are its temple. (23) The City does not need the sun or the moon to shine on it, for the glory of God gives it light, and the Lamb is its lamp. (24) The nations will walk by its light, and the kings of the earth will bring their splendor into it. (25) On no day will its gates ever be shut, for there will be no night there. (26) The glory and honor of the nations will be brought into it. (27) Nothing impure will ever enter it, nor will anyone who does what is shameful or deceitful, but only those whose names are written in The Lamb's Book of Life.

The glory of God will be the light source of this city. Light bulbs will never have to be replaced, generators will never burn up. There will never be any pollution from this power source. It will never have to be replenished.

The nations refers to the Gentiles and they will bring their glory and honor into the city. There will be nothing allowed in the city that is impure, shameful, or deceitful. The only ones allowed in the City will be those whose names are written in The Lamb's Book of Life.

This description of the New Jerusalem presents an awesome picture of the glory of God, but we cannot even imagine the things that God has prepared for us. But, you have got to believe to get there.

John 14:6 Jesus answered, "I am the Way, the Truth, and the Life. No one comes to the Father except through me!"

I believe that this is the most profound statement that Jesus made in His ministry. If you do not believe this statement exactly as it is written, you might as well quit playing religious games and concentrate on the things of the world.

The unmistakable central message of this passage of scripture is Jesus Christ as the Lamb of God. The purity of this Holy City of God coming down from Heaven, is guaranteed by not allowing anyone or anything in it that would defile its purity and beauty.

John was allowed to witness a new creation by God, designed by God, made perfect by God and working as God intended for it to work for His people. God revealed to John all the splendor of life that He has for His people whose names are written in "The Lamb's Book of Life".

Revelation 22:1 Then the angel showed me the river of water of life, as clear as crystal, flowing from the throne of God and of The Lamb.

The water of life represents the purity, the power, and the holiness of eternal life in the New Jerusalem. The fact that the water of life flows from the throne of God and of The Lamb, proves that Jesus is still at the right hand of God.

Revelation 22:2 Down the middle of the great street of the city, on each side of the river stood the tree of life, bearing twelve crops of fruit, yielding its fruit every month. And the leaves of the tree are for the healing of the nations.

Whether this is one large tree and a small stream of whether there is more than one tree and they are on both sides of the stream is not of great importance. What is important is that this tree of life refers to the "Word of God", and that it will never return to Him void. It will always produce fruit. Even in this new and beautiful city, God will continue to provide the needs of His people.

Revelation 22:3 No longer will there be any curse. The throne of God and of The Lamb will be in the city and the servants will serve Him.

Matthew 4:10 Jesus is high on the mountain and is being tempted by Satan. Jesus said to him, "Away from me, Satan! For it is written: Worship the Lord, your God and serve Him only."

Worship and serve are synonymous in these two passages. When we worship God, we are serving Him, and when we serve Him, we are worshipping Him. It is kind of like a horse and buggy, they just kinda go together, one compliments the other.

Revelation 22:4 They will see His face, and His name will be written on their foreheads.

Seeing the face of God was something that was not possible before the resurrection of the saints. Being able to see the face of God, demonstrates that His people have been made perfectly holy by the grace of God.

Revelation 22:5 There will be no more night. They will not need the light of the lamp, or the light of the sun, for the Lord God will give them light. And they will reign forever and ever.

The New Jerusalem will be an amazing, beautiful city. The translucent materials that make up the New Holy City will allow light to stream through all of the various colors, there will be no shadows anywhere. The sun and the moon will be no more. The glory of God will light up the city, and all of the saints will reign with Jesus forever.

Revelation 22:6 The angel said to me, "These words are trustworthy and true. The Lord, the God of the spirits of the prophets, sent His angel to show His servants the things that must soon take place.

God has put down evil and has judged Satan and all of his followers. No trace of sin will taint the New Holy City of Jerusalem. Where there was once death, there will now be resurrection of life forever. Where there was once judgement, now there is redemption. Where there was once darkness, now there is eternal light. Joy will replace sorrow. All of the Saints will worship and serve God the Father, God the Son and God the Holy Spirit.

The servants will be transformed into the likeness of God. They will be identified with His name on their foreheads. This is more proof that we will have some form of a body. It would seem that it would be pretty hard to put a name on the forehead of a ghost or spirit.

Revelation 22:7 Jesus is Coming. "Behold, I am coming soon! Blessed is he who keeps the words of the prophecy in this book."

This verse is one of the master keys to Revelation. You must believe that Jesus is coming again. Blessed is the one who believes that this prophecy will be fulfilled. We may not understand completely how or when, but by the same faith that we know that we are saved into the Kingdom of God, we must believe the prophecy of this Book.

If this prophecy is not going to be fulfilled to its fullest extent, why would Jesus make this statement?

Revelation 22:16 "I, Jesus, have sent my angel to give you this testimony."

If you don't believe Jesus, who do you believe?

Remember in **Revelation 11:1 – 12** John prophesied that two of God's prophets would witness for God for forty two months and then be killed by the beast. Their bodies would lie in the streets for three and a half days, while the world watched and gloated over them. Then a breath of life from God entered into them and they stood on their feet and terror struck those who saw them. Then to add more fear to their enemies, God said to them, "Come up here," and they immediately ascended into Heaven to be with God.

Do you believe that God told John that He was going to let these dummies invent satellite television so they could witness this event, or did John believe what God told him on faith?

Revelation 22:8 – 9 (8) I, John, am the one who heard and saw these things. And when I had heard and seen them, I fell down at the feet of the angel who had been showing them to me. (9) But, he said to me, "Do not do it! I am a fellow servant with you and with your brothers, the prophets and all who keep the words of this Book. Worship God!"

How would you have liked to have been sitting on the Isle of Patmos with John as God was scrolling all of this across the screen of His television? Each scene was more spectacular than the one that preceded it.

The elected people of God are not to worship any being other than God. No spiritual being, or angel, or Mary, whether in Heaven or on earth is to be worshipped. "Only God."

Matthew 23:8 – 10 (8) But, you are not to be called, "Rabbi", for you have only one master and you are all brothers. (9) And, do not call anyone on earth, "father", for you have one Father and He is in Heaven. (10) Nor, are you to be called, "teacher", for you have on teacher, The Christ.

This is where I have a hard time understanding the rituals and the rules of the Catholic Church. It appears to me that they believe that the Pope and the other leaders of their church are somehow on the same playing field of God.

It has been stated several times in Revelation that we are to "Worship God Only". No one else is worthy of worship.

How much plainer could Jesus have made it in these three verses that we are not to honor humans by calling them names that are associated with God.?

From **Matthew 23:13** through **Matthew 23:29** Jesus uses this same statement seven times. "Woe to you, teachers of the law and Pharisees, you hypocrites."

It seems to me that Jesus had a message for the religious leaders of His day. This still holds true for today and forever. I believe that Hell will burn a little hotter when someone gets there that leads any of God's people astray.

Revelation 22:10 - 11 (10) Then he told me, "Do not seal up the words of this prophecy, because the time is near. (11) Let him who does wrong, continue to do wrong; let him who is vile, continue to be vile; let him who does right, continue to do right; and let him who is holy continue to be holy."

In giving John those instructions the angel is stating that things on earth will not change until the Coming of the Lord. The evil and the vile will continue to be evil and vile and the good and the holy needs to continue to be holy and good.

The call to repent of our sins will cease one day. Our human intentions to change will never have another chance to become reality. People will not suddenly become righteous in the last days. There will be many that will deny Him until they see Him coming with His army of saints. Then they will say, "Oh, Hell, I didn't think that I would ever see this day."

Revelation 22:12 – 16 (12) "Behold, I am coming soon! My reward is with me, and I will give to everyone according to what he has done. (13) I am the Alpha and the Omega, the First and the Last, the beginning and the End. (14) Blessed are those who wash their robes, that they may have the right to the tree of life, and may go through the gates into the city. (15) Outside are the dogs, those who practice magic arts, the sexually immoral, the murderers, the idolaters, and everyone who loves and practices falsehood. (16) I, Jesus, have sent my angel to give you this testimony for the churches. I am the Root and the Offspring of David, and the Bright and Morning Star. Behold, I am coming soon!"

This is the third of three times that Jesus makes this statement in this last chapter. He is saying, undeniably and unequivocally that He is coming back.

"Blessed are those who wash their robes", is translated in the King James Version as, "Blessed are those who keep His commandments".

If our robes are washed spotless and as white as snow, then we will be keeping God's commandments and doing His will. If we keep God's commandments and do His will, then our robes will be washed as white as snow. The important thing is that the believers are now justified to enter the Holy City and they have a right to the tree of life.

The unbelievers are described as "dogs" and will not be allowed to enter into the Holy City. The word "dogs" here does not refer to the animal, but to the sinner who does not qualify to be in the presence of God. They have lived a life of immorality and lies and their lives have not been touched by the "Amazing Grace" of God.

As we all know, the darkest hour of the day is just before morning begins to break. This is how Jesus will appear when He returns again. He will be like the morning star, the brightest thing in the sky. All of the world will see Him when He returns, in all of His glory.

This is the first reference of the churches, since the messages to the seven churches in Revelation 2 and 3. The reason for this is that the "church" was raptured and did not have to suffer through the Tribulation years.

In verse thirteen Jesus makes virtually the same statement that the Lord God made in **Revelation 1:8** "I am the Alpha and the Omega," says the Lord God, "who is and who was, and who is to come, the Almighty."

Revelation 22:13 "I am the Alpha and the Omega, the First and the Last, the Beginning and the End."

God the Father, God the Son, and God the Holy Spirit, this is the Holy Trinity, all the same, but all different. It blows our human mind that we cannot figure this out. We just have to accept the fact that this is who God is.

Revelation 22:17 The spirit and the bride say, "Come"! And, let him who hears say "Come"! Whoever is thirsty, let him come, and whoever wishes, let him take the free gift of the water of life.

This is one power packed verse. The Holy Spirit says "Come", the bride (the church) says "Come". This means that everyone who hears the Gospel and accepts Jesus Christ as their Lord and Savior should invite others to come to know and accept Jesus as their Lord and Savior. It does not matter where you are or what the circumstances are, God will give you the tools that you need to witness for Him.

Acts 1:7 – 8 (7) He said to them: "It is not for you to know the times or the dates the Father has set by His own authority. (8) But, you will receive power when the Holy Spirit comes on you; and you will be my witnesses in Jerusalem, and in all Judea, and Samaria, and to the ends of the earth.

Acts 2:1 – 4 (1) When the day of Pentecost came, they were all together in one place. (2) Suddenly, a sound like the blowing of a violent wind came from Heaven and filled the whole house where they were sitting. (3) They saw what seemed to be tongues of fire that separated and came to rest on each of them. (4) All of them were filled with the Holy Spirit, and they began to speak in other tongues, as the spirit enabled them.

In the next nine verses Luke tells us that these disciples went out into the streets of Jerusalem and began to preach to every Jew in the city in their own language. They did not need a crash course in foreign language. The Holy Spirit enabled them to witness to every Jew from every nation under the sun. The spirit is given to all believers. Without this giving and being filled with the Holy Spirit of God upon the church, the people are never brought to faith in Jesus Christ.

When the Spirit is at work, Jesus Christ is proclaimed. The Spirit led Peter to preach about Jesus, not about the Spirit. Later the Holy Spirit inspired Luke to write the Book of Acts. Verbal revelation without any experience of the Spirit as dead.

If you talk the walk, you must walk the talk. What monkey see – monkey do, not, what monkey hear – monkey do.

"Come"!! This action packed word is what God the Father, God the Son, and God the Holy Spirit has been urging people to do from Genesis to Revelation. There are three conditions that we must meet to receive God's gracious offer of eternal life:

(1) We must recognize our need symbolized by being "thirsty".

(2) We must be willing to repent of our sins. (Turn away from sin)

(3) We must turn to Jesus and accept Him as our Lord and Savior.

The "Old, Old Story", is still good news today. The invitation is still open to everyone who is willing to turn to Jesus and follow Him.

Revelation 22:18 – 20 (18)"I warn everyone who hears the words of this Book: If anyone adds anything to them, God will add to him the plagues described in this Book. (19) If anyone takes words away from this Book of Prophecy, God will take away from him, his share in the tree of life, which is described in this Book. (20) He who testifies to these things says, "Yes, I am coming soon!" Amen! Come Lord Jesus!

Tampering with the word of God is a tremendous sin.

Deuteronomy 4:2 Do not add to what I command you, and do not subtract from it, but keep the commands of the Lord your God, that I give you.

Deuteronomy 12:32 See that you do all that I command you: do not add to it or take away from it.

Proverbs 30:5 – 6 (5) Every word of God is flawless; he is a shield to those who take refuge in Him. (6) Do not add to His words, or He will rebuke you and prove you a liar.

This is one of the biggest fallacies of preachers, teachers and all church leaders of today. Many of them do not preach or teach the alternative to salvation. They preach and teach what they think their congregations want "to hear, how great we are". Not "How Great Thou Art".

Many churches are better known for trying to provide solutions to the economic social ills of the world, that for preaching the Whole

Gospel. These things are well and good and God expects us to help others in need. But, they will not buy you salvation.

When you ask the question, "Are you saved?" Many people will answer, "I think I am," or "I hope I am." You have to know that you know that Jesus Christ is your Lord and Savior.

John 3:16 For God so loved the world that He gave His only begotten son, so that whosoever believes in Him shall not perish, but have everlasting life.

John 14:6 Jesus answered, "I am the way, the truth and the life. No one comes to the Father except through me!!"

There is on other way. You accept Jesus Christ as your Lord and Savior, or you burn in Hell forever and ever.

John closed this great Book of the Bible with a simple prayer. **Revelation 22:21** "The grace of the Lord Jesus be with God's people. Amen."

The Bible does not present in any other Book the contrasting picture of the awfulness of sin and its divine judgements or the blessings of being a child of God through Jesus Christ, His Son.

All of the prophetic revelations from Genesis to Jude are climaxed in the Book of Revelation.

The City of Jerusalem is mentioned "888" times in the Bible. Do you think this prophecy won't come true?

If you died today, where would you spend eternity? Hell is Real!!!!

The Central Teaching of Revelation

Born once: from the cradle

Die twice: sinner: Dead on arrival. Lake of Fire. To the grave.......to the flames of Hell

Born Twice: from the cradle to the cross. Eternal Life

Die once: Christian: I am not here! Resurrected by the Blood of Jesus Christ

The choice is yours, you will make one!

Appendix A

Chapters 16, 17, 18, and 19 are the hardest chapters in Revelation for many people to believe. They will tell you that Babylon has already been destroyed. But, even if you believe that Babylon was destroyed by invading armies, God did not destroy it.

The antichrist will be the most powerful man in the world during the first three and a half years of the Tribulation. He will control all of the money, people and equipment in the world. He will have people working day and night seven days a week to build the city of Babylon.

Isaiah 13:19 may be the most revealing verse in the Bible to prophesy the happenings in these four chapters. Babylon, the jewel of the kingdoms, the pride and glory of the Babylonians, will be overthrown by God, like Sodom and Gomorrah. God destroyed Sodom and Gomorrah in one day by fire. He can surely destroy Babylon by fire and earthquake.

Appendix B

Is kissing a statue of the Mother Mary or any other statue before you pray to Jesus or God or whoever the Catholics pray to as their god a sign of idol worship?

The Lord's Prayer: Matthew 6:9 – 13 (9) Our Father which art in heaven, Hallowed be thy name. (10) Thy kingdom come. Thy will be done on earth, as it is in Heaven. (11) Give us this day our daily bread. (12) And forgive us our debts, as we forgive our debtors. (13) And lead us not into temptation but deliver us from evil. For thine is the kingdom and the power and the glory forever. Amen!!

Look closely at verse ten, Jesus is telling us how we should live our lives on this earth. We are supposed to be different from the world. How can you convince someone to come to Jesus as their Lord and Savior if they see you doing the same things that they do?

Verse thirteen says, "And lead us not into temptation, but deliver us from evil."

Why did Jesus tell us that we should ask not to be led into the temptations of the world? If everyone is going to Heaven and live forever with God, why did Jesus tell us to pray to be different from the world? Did Jesus think that the world was not evil and we should not be worried about being caught up in the evil things of the world? It seems pretty clear to me that Jesus thought that the world was evil and that we should not be tempted to be drawn into it.

So why do I have to bow down before a statue that is as dead as any rock or any other god that heathens pray to and ask them to deliver my prayer to my God, who is alive in Heaven and hears my prayers as well as He hears anyone else's prayers? I don't even have to kiss the feet of a statue of Mother Mary to get my prayers heard in Heaven.

www.ingramcontent.com/pod-product-compliance
Lightning Source LLC
Chambersburg PA
CBHW022058050726
47591CB00002B/597

* 9 7 8 1 9 6 4 8 1 0 3 1 7 *